D1633673

Essential
England

AAA Publishing 1000 AAA Drive, Heathrow, Florida 32746

England: Regions and Best places to see

Original text by Terry Marsh
Updated by Robin Barton

American editor: G.K. Sharman

Edited, designed and produced by AA Publishing
© Automobile Association Developments Limited 2007
Maps © Automobile Association Developments Limited 2007

ISBN-13: 978-1-59508-176-6
ISBN-10: 1-59508-176-3

Automobile Association Developments Limited retains the copyright in the original
edition © 2001 and in all subsequent editions, reprints and amendments

All rights reserved. No part of this publication may be reproduced, stored in a
retrieval system, or transmitted in any form or by any means – electronic,
photocopying, recording or otherwise – unless the written permission of the
publishers has been obtained beforehand.

The contents of this publication are believed correct at the time of printing.
Nevertheless, the publishers cannot be held responsible for any errors or
omissions or for changes in the details given in this guide or for the
consequences of any reliance on the information provided by the same.

Published in the United States by AAA Publishing,
1000 AAA Drive, Heathrow, Florida 32746
Published in the United Kingdom by AA Publishing

Colour separation: MRM Graphics Ltd
Printed and bound in Italy by Printer Trento S.r.l.

A02694

OS Ordnance Survey This product includes mapping data licensed from Ordnance
Survey® with the permission of the Controller of Her Majesty's
Stationery Office.
© Crown copyright 2007. All rights reserved. Licence number 399221

About this book

Symbols are used to denote the following categories:

- ✚ map reference to maps on cover
- ✉ address or location
- ☎ telephone number
- 🕐 opening times
- ✋ admission charge
- 🍴 restaurant or café on premises or nearby
- Ⓟ nearest underground train station
- 🚌 nearest bus/tram route
- 🚆 nearest overground train station
- ⛴ nearest ferry stop
- ❓ other practical information
- ℹ tourist information office
- ➤ indicates the page where you will find a fuller description

This book is divided into five sections.

The essence of England pages 6–19
Introduction; Features; Food and Drink; Short Break including the 10 Essentials

Planning pages 20–33
Before You Go; Getting There; Getting Around; Being There

Best places to see pages 34–55
The unmissable highlights of any visit to England

Best things to do pages 56–73
Good places to have lunch; where to take the children; best houses and gardens; top outdoor activities; best places to stay and more

Exploring pages 74–187
The best places to visit in England, organized by area

Maps
All map references are to the maps on the covers. For example, Oxford has the reference ✚ 14R– indicating the grid square in which it is to be found

Prices
An indication of the cost of restaurants and cafés at attractions is given by £ signs: **£££** denotes higher prices, **££** denotes average prices, **£** denotes lower prices

Hotel prices
Price are per room per night: **£** budget (under £70); **££** moderate (£70–£150); **£££** expensive to luxury (over £150)

Restaurant prices
Price for a three-course meal per person without drinks: **£** budget (under £20); **££** moderate (£20–£30); **£££** expensive (over £30)

Contents

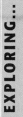

BEST THINGS TO DO

56 – 73

EXPLORING...

74 – 187

The essence of...

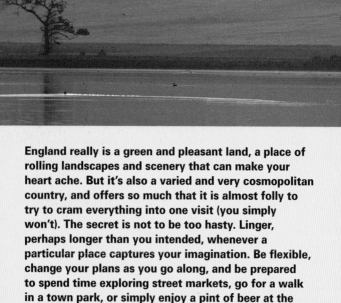

England really is a green and pleasant land, a place of rolling landscapes and scenery that can make your heart ache. But it's also a varied and very cosmopolitan country, and offers so much that it is almost folly to try to cram everything into one visit (you simply won't). The secret is not to be too hasty. Linger, perhaps longer than you intended, whenever a particular place captures your imagination. Be flexible, change your plans as you go along, and be prepared to spend time exploring street markets, go for a walk in a town park, or simply enjoy a pint of beer at the local pub.

THE ESSENCE OF ENGLAND

features

For many visitors it is hard to comprehend the variety England has to offer, from its charming country villages to the magnificent monuments of its great cities; it's a place of extremes but also seems very homogeneous and united.

Today England is a world leader in art, music and fashion. Politically and economically it is still a major player, as a part of the United Kingdom. There is a great feeling of openness, of a willingness to share England's heritage, whatever form it takes, with visitors and local people alike.

But England is also very European, in spite of the political bickering that goes on. Gone is the arrogance of imperialism; instead there is a recognition that England is one among many on the world's stage, with a role for everyone. It is a more worldly, more enterprising place that above all has a developing pride in its history and its place in the world.

THE COUNTRY

● England is the largest political division of the United Kingdom of Great Britain and Northern Ireland.

● It is a highly industrialized and agriculturally developed country, densely populated and rich in history.

● London, the capital, is also by far England's largest city, with over 7 million inhabitants.

● Birmingham in central England, the next largest city, has around a million inhabitants.

● Northern England boasts a clutch of cities with around 500,000 inhabitants, including Leeds, Manchester, Liverpool, Bradford, Sheffield and Newcastle. In the southwest, Bristol and Plymouth are the largest centres of population.

THE ECONOMY
● England's most important exports are oil, gas, technology and financial services.
● 50 years ago the most important exports were coal, iron, steel, shipbuilding, textiles and pottery.

A FEW FACTS AND FIGURES
Area: 50,331sq miles
(130,357sq km)
Currency: pound (£) sterling
Population: approx 50 million in 2004
Language: English, with many varied dialects. Several hundred minority languages are also spoken

OPEN SPACES
● In England, nine National Parks, including the newest in the New Forest, offer almost 5,000sq miles (13,000sq km) of countryside, protected for their scenic and recreational value.
● There are also more than 40 designated Areas of Outstanding Natural Beauty (AONB), with a similar protected status.
● Spread across the English countryside is a massive network of thousands of miles of footpaths, bridleways (open to horses and cyclists) and byways.
● Most towns and cities have formal parks in or near their centres, while in the surrounding areas you'll find country parks, where there is a less formal environment, and a greater chance of seeing some wildlife.

food & drink

It is virtually impossible to identify an English cuisine in the way that you might a French style – yet if such a thing exists, it is probably associated with good, plain cooking of fresh ingredients. In the mid-20th century it became characterized as

Come in for
A GOOD POT OF TEA
AND
Try Our
CREAM TEAS & CRAB SANDWICHES

'meat and two veg' or 'school dinners', a sometimes affectionate reflection on the fare served up in school canteens.

For many, 'English' means hearty meat pies, soggy vegetables and heavy desserts such as bread-and-butter-pudding, inevitably served with custard. In recent years 'modern English' has taken a lighter look at the old favourites, and you'll find new takes on traditional menus in pubs and restaurants across the country. And don't forget the sandwich was an English invention.

CHEESE

Cheeses are perhaps the most readily identifiable regional specialities. Cheddar (originally from Somerset) is the dominant style, but avoid the plastic supermarket variety and seek out the traditionally made from somewhere like Chewton Dairy in the Mendip Hills. Cheshire, Lancashire and Wensleydale are crumbly white cheeses, the prefix 'tasty' often used to

describe sharper, more mature varieties. They go very well with fruitcake. Central England produces the orangey-coloured Red Leicester, the smooth and herby Sage Derby and, most famously, the mature, blue-veined Stilton (delicious with a crisp apple). You'll find the best ranges of cheese are

available at specialist delicatessens and farm stalls in traditional markets.

MEAT AND FISH

When it comes to meat, England is usually associated with beef, whether grilled as steak, roasted as a joint and served with Yorkshire pudding (savoury batter), or cooked slowly with root vegetables in a stew. Look for local specialities of sausages; Cumberland are long and spicy, Lincolnshire, mild and herb flavoured. Black pudding, made with offal, is popular in the northern counties. Lamb too, is a popular ingredient but vegetarian food is also well established.

As you might expect, seafood is important. On the east coast, Craster is famous for its smoked kippers and Whitby for its crabs. In the

southeast, whelks, jellied eels, cockles and mussels are all popular. Wherever you are in England, you're never far from a fish and chip shop, selling cod or haddock fried in batter and served with chips. They're best eaten straight from the wrapper, and sprinkled with salt and vinegar.

CAKES AND ALE

Tea time may no longer be *the* afternoon event, but the English retain a fondness for cakes. A Lancashire Eccles cake is sweet mincemeat wrapped in pastry; gingerbread in Grasmere, Cumbria is a delicious, thin, crumbly affair more like a biscuit; and Derbyshire's Bakewell Pudding is commonly recognized as a jam tart topped with sponge.

There are English wines, though the climate means only the whites are generally up to world standards. In beers, you will find the global brands

available alongside the peculiarly English ales. Served in pint glasses, the best of these are the 'real ales', which continue to mature in their barrels after leaving the brewery. The dominant varieties are bitters, such as Tetleys or Courage Best; the darker and usually less strong milds (Banks's is very popular in central England); and the pale ales, a wide range of which are produced locally. In western England, traditional cider is still the favourite drink for many locals.

short break

If you have only a short time to visit England and would like to take home some unforgettable memories, you can do something local to capture the real flavour of the country. The following suggestions are a wide range of sights and experiences that won't take very long, won't cost too much and will make your visit very special.

● **Take a ride in a London cab** – ask the cabbie to show you as many of the sights of London as he can in an hour. Avoid rush hours and try fixing a price first.

● **Try real ale** or cider, particularly in a traditional English pub. Freehouses often stock interesting beers from independent local breweries.

● **Visit a cathedral** – every one is an architectural marvel, and a peaceful place where you can slow things down for a while.

● **Watch a traditional ceremony.** Changing the Guard is the most famous daily event in London.

● **Explore the Lake District** – there is so much beautiful countryside in England, but the Lake District crams a lot in a small space (➤ 44–45).

● **Try fish and chips** – not really the English staple diet, but very filling.

● **Visit a stately home** – found all over the country, but allow enough time to see everything.

● **Go shopping in a street market** – markets are a traditional feature of many English towns. Increasing in popularity, even in cities, are farmers' markets which often sell organic and local produce. Check local press for details. Whether you buy anything or not, you're sure to be entertained by the market traders' banter.

● **Go to a show in London.** Try theatre box offices first or legitimate ticket agents such as Ticketmaster (www.ticketmaster.co.uk). Discounted tickets for same day performances can also be bought at the offical booths in Leicester Square and Canary Wharf.

● **See cities** such as Bath, Oxford, Cambridge and York from the top of a double-decker tour bus.

● **Visit a village fête or agricultural show** – always a great day out, with cattle shows, dog trials, folk dancing, cookery competitions, craft displays and activities for the whole family.

● **Visit an industrial museum** – there are many around the country, but the Ironbridge Gorge (► 124–125) in Shropshire is looked on as the cradle of the Industrial Revolution.

Planning

Before You Go

WHEN TO GO

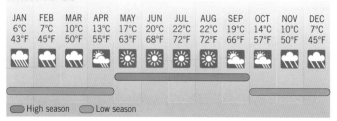

JAN	FEB	MAR	APR	MAY	JUN	JUL	AUG	SEP	OCT	NOV	DEC
6°C	7°C	10°C	13°C	17°C	20°C	22°C	22°C	19°C	14°C	10°C	7°C
43°F	45°F	50°F	55°F	63°F	68°F	72°F	72°F	66°F	57°F	50°F	45°F

High season   Low season

England is a destination with all-year-round appeal, but for the best weather, visit during the summer months (May to September). Daylight hours are longest in May and June, peaking at 17 hours daily. In the winter it gets dark at about 4pm. Thanks to a maritime climate, weather patterns across England are variable, but the Gulf Stream ensures that Britain is warmer than other countries on the same latitude, with temperatures rarely falling much below freezing in winter.

Although some attractions, such as a few National Trust properties, close during the winter (typically from November to Easter), an off-peak visit should mean lower accommodation prices (outside the cities) and less-crowded sights.

WHAT YOU NEED

● Required
○ Suggested
▲ Not required

Some countries require a passport to remain valid for a minimum period (usually at least six months) beyond the date of entry – contact their consulate or embassy or your travel agent for details.

	UK	Germany	USA	Netherlands	Spain
Passport (or National Identity Card where applicable)	▲	▲	●	●	●
Visa (regulations can change – check before you travel)	▲	▲	▲	▲	▲
Onward or Return Ticket	▲	○	○	○	○
Health Inoculations (tetanus and polio)	▲	▲	▲	▲	▲
Health Documentation (► 23, Health Advice)	▲	●	●	●	●
Travel Insurance	○	○	○	○	○
Driving Licence (national)	●	●	●	●	●
Car Insurance Certificate	▲	●	●	●	●
Car Registration Document	▲	●	●	●	●

ADVANCE PLANNING
WEBSITES
www.travelbritain.org
www.visitbritain.com
www.english-heritage.org.uk
www.bbc.co.uk
www.thetrainline.com
www.theaa.com
www.pti.org.uk
www.nationalparks.gov.uk
www.fco.gov.uk
www.metoffice.com
www.nationaltrust.org.uk

TOURIST OFFICES AT HOME
In the USA
Suite 701,
551 Fifth Avenue,
New York,
NY 10176
☎ 212/986-2266

HEALTH ADVICE
Medical insurance The EHIC (European Health Insurance Card) allows EU nationals free or reduced cost medical treatment in other EU nations. It is free to apply for the card (**www.**ehic.org.uk). Private medical insurance is still advised, and is essential for all other visitors.

Dental treatment Emergency dental treatment may be available free of charge if you can find a National Health dentist willing to treat you. A list can be found in the Yellow Pages. Dental treatment should be covered by private medical insurance.

TIME DIFFERENCES

GMT	British Summer	Germany	USA (NY)	Netherlands	Spain
12 noon	1PM	1–2PM	7AM	1PM	1PM

England is on Greenwich Mean Time (GMT) in winter, but from late March until late October, British Summer Time (BST, i.e.GMT+1) operates.

WHAT'S ON WHEN

January *Lord Mayor's Parade*, London.

February *Chinese New Year* celebrations, Liverpool, Manchester and London.

March *Irish Festival*, Manchester
Crufts Dog Show, NEC, Birmingham.

April *Oxford and Cambridge Boat Race*, River Thames, London. (Sometimes held in March.)
Padstow Fish and Ships Festival Bottle Kicking and Hare Pie, Padstow.
Scrambling, Hallaton, near Medbourne, Leicestershire.
London Marathon, London.
Shakespeare's birthday, Stratford-upon-Avon, Warwickshire.

May *Furry Dance*, Helston, Cornwall.
Lancashire Clog Dancing Festival, Accrington, Lancashire.
Royal Windsor Horse Show, Windsor Home Park.

Chelsea Flower Show, London.
Cheese Rolling Festival, Coopers Hill, Gloucestershire.

June *Trooping the Colour*, Horse Guards Parade, London.
Three Counties Show, Malvern, Worcestershire.
East of England Show, Peterborough, Cambridgeshire.
Wimbledon Tennis Championships.
Appleby Horse Fair, Appleby-in-Westmorland, Cumbria.
Glastonbury Festival, Glastonbury Somerset.

July *Farnborough International Airshow*, Hampshire.
The Great Yorkshire Show, Harrogate, Yorkshire.
Henley Royal Regatta, Henley-on-

NATIONAL HOLIDAYS

JAN	FEB	MAR	APR	MAY	JUN	JUL	AUG	SEP	OCT	NOV	DEC
1		(2)	(2)	2			1				2

1 Jan	New Year's Day
March/April	Good Friday and Easter Monday
First Mon in May	May Day Bank Holiday
Last Mon in May	Late May Bank Holiday
Last Mon in August	August Bank Holiday Monday
25 Dec	Christmas Day
26 Dec	Boxing Day

Almost all attractions close on Christmas Day. On other holidays some attractions open, often with reduced hours. There are no general rules regarding the opening times of restaurants and shops, so check before making a special journey.

Thames, Oxfordshire.
Royal International Agricultural Show, Stoneleigh, Warwickshire
Royal International Air Tattoo, Fairford, Gloucestershire.

August *International Beatles Week*, Liverpool.
Gay Fest, Manchester
Rush-bearing ceremony, Grasmere, Cumbria.
Southport Flower Show, Southport, Lancashire
Billingham International Folklore Festival, Cleveland.
Notting Hill Carnival, London.
Grasmere Sports, Cumbria.
Cowes Regatta, Isle of Wight.

September *Artsfest*, Birmingham
Blackpool Illuminations, Blackpool

Great North Run, Gateshead
Southampton International Boat Show, Southampton, Hampshire.
Biggest Liar in the World Competition, Santon Bridge, Cumbria.
Widecombe Fair, Widecombe-in-the-Moor, Devon.

October *Goose Fair*, Nottingham.
World Conker Championships, Ashton, Northamptonshire.

November *Guy Fawkes Night* (bonfires and firework displays throughout the country).
London to Brighton Veteran Car Run.
Lord Mayor's Show, London.

December *Mummers Play and Morris Dancing*, Northamptonshire.

Getting There

BY AIR

There are direct flights to England from all over the world. Most long-haul flights arrive at London Heathrow or London Gatwick, while London's other three airports (Stansted, Luton and London City) serve mainly short-haul destinations. International flights also operate from Birmingham International, Manchester, Southampton, Leeds and Bradford. Low-cost flights operate to some local airports.

BY SEA

Ferries serve England from Ireland and many ports in continental Europe. The 24-mile (38km) Channel Tunnel provides a fast train link with France via Eurostar (see below). The train service for cars, caravans and motorcycles through the tunnel is operated by Eurotunnel.

BY RAIL

Eurostar trains run beween Waterloo (London) and Ashford (Kent), in England;

Paris and Lille, in France, and Brussels, in Belgium. Passports are required and passengers must clear customs.

DRIVING

Driving is on the left.
Speed limit on motorways and dual carriageways: **70mph (112kph)**
Speed limit on main roads: **50–60mph (80–100kph)**
Speed limit on minor roads: **30–40mph (50–65kph)**

Seat belts must be worn in front seats at all times and in rear seats where available.

Random breath tests are carried out frequently, especially late at night. The limit is 35 micrograms of alcohol in 100ml of breath.

Fuel is sold in litres and available as unleaded (95 octane), super unleaded (98 octane) and diesel. Other than in the centre of cities, petrol stations are numerous. Petrol stations are typically open

6am–10pm (and 24 hours on major roads) but don't rely on these times in rural areas. Fuel is very heavily taxed, making it more expensive than in Europe or the USA. Prices vary slightly across the country.

If you break down driving your own car and are a member of an AA-affiliated motoring club, you can call the AA (☎ 0800 887 766 toll free). If your car is rented, follow the instructions given in the documentation; most rental firms provide a rescue service.

Getting Around

PUBLIC TRANSPORT
INTERNAL FLIGHTS

Internal flights serve the business community, but their often prohibitive cost means that English people rarely use them for 'social' travel. Major British cities – Edinburgh, Glasgow, Cardiff, Belfast – are well served.

TRAINS

All the major towns and cities are connected by fast and frequent services, but intermediate stations tend to be served only by slower services. Train lines radiate from London, and 'cross-country ' services between provincial cities can be more difficult. The complex nature of the rail system's privatization in the 1990s means that a variety of differing operators may run trains on the same routes. There is a rail enquiry line and website to help you plan your journey (☎ 0845 748 4950;

www.nationalrail.co.uk) and tickets can be bought in advance and over the phone. Tickets are much more expensive if you leave it until your day of travel to buy them and if you travel during rush hour.

BUSES

These come in all shapes and sizes, providing cheap and effective local transport, either in urban areas or connecting small towns and villages in rural areas. Bus companies are privately owned but local authorities often subsidize routes in remote places. A few cities, notably Manchester, Sheffield and Wolverhampton, now run efficient tram services as an alternative to local buses.

COACHES

Travel by coach – a long-distance 'bus', and invariably more comfortable – is a slower option than train travel, but its relative cheapness makes it popular with the budget traveller. The main provider is National Express

(www.nationalexpress.com) who serves most towns and cities.

CAR RENTAL

The leading international car rental companies have offices at all airports and you can book a car in advance. Local companies offer competitive rates and will deliver a car to the airport.

TAXIS

Anywhere in England you can telephone a private taxi company to collect you from where you are and take you to wherever you want to go. Your taxi may be any type of car, though London's famous 'black cabs' are increasingly found in other towns and cities.

CONCESSIONS
Students and senior citizens
Senior Citizens and holders of an International Student Identity Card will be able to obtain some concessions. There are a handful of good youth hostels in London and around the country, although you don't have to be young to stay in them.
Children Concessions for children are usually available when paying for accommodation, travel or admission to an attraction. However, age limits do vary considerably.

Being There

TOURIST OFFICES
REGIONAL TOURIST BOARDS

Every town in England also has a local tourist information centre.

- Cumbria Tourist Board, Ashleigh, Holly Road, Windermere, Cumbria ☎ 01539 444444
- East of England Tourist Board, Toppesfield Hall, Hadleigh, Suffolk ☎ 01473 822922
- Heart of England Tourist Board, Woodside, Larkhill Road, Worcester ☎ 01905 763436
- London Tourist Board, 26 Grosvenor Gardens, London
- North West Tourist Board, Swan House, Swan Meadow Road, Wigan
- Northumbria Tourist Board, Aykley Heads, Durham ☎ 01271 336182
- South East England Tourist Board, The Old Brew House, Warwick Park, Tunbridge Wells, Kent ☎ 01892 540766
- Tourism South East, 40 Chamberlayne Road, Eastleigh, Hampshire ☎ 023 8062 5400
- Southwest Tourism, Woodwater Park, Exeter, Devon ☎ 01392 360050
- Yorkshire Tourist Board, 312 Tadcaster Road, York YO2 2HF ☎ 01904 707961

EMBASSIES AND CONSULATES
Germany ☎ 0207 824 1300
USA ☎ 020 7499 9000
Netherlands ☎ 020 7590 3200
Spain ☎ 0207 235 5555

TELEPHONES

The traditional red phone boxes are now rare; instead, kiosks come in a wide variety of different designs, depending on which phone company is operating them. Pay phones are either coin-operated and take 10p, 20p, 50p and £1 coins or some take credit cards. Other phone booths use pre-paid cards which are readily available in shops. To call the operator dial 100.

EMERGENCY TELEPHONE NUMBERS
Police: 999
Fire: 999
Ambulance: 999

INTERNATIONAL DIALLING CODES
From England to:
Germany: 00 49
USA/Canada: 00 1
Australia: 00 61
Netherlands: 00 31
Spain: 00 34

OPENING HOURS

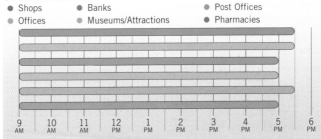

- Shops
- Offices
- Banks
- Museums/Attractions
- Post Offices
- Pharmacies

9 AM	10 AM	11 AM	12 PM	1 PM	2 PM	3 PM	4 PM	5 PM	6 PM

The times shown above are traditional opening hours. Many shops throughout England, especially those in the cities and large towns (but increasingly elsewhere) open for longer hours, many of them now on Sundays too. High Street banks are generally open Saturday mornings and bureaux de change are open daily. Museums and visitor attractions close for one day a week, and often on special occasions. It is always wise to check the times by telephoning first. When pharmacies are closed you'll find a sign in the window giving details of the nearest one that is on 24-hour duty.

POSTAL SERVICES

Post offices tend to be open Mon–Fri 9–5:30, Sat 9–1, though there are local variations. Post boxes, which are generally red, come in many shapes and sizes, and provide a fascinating study in themselves. Many date from Victorian times.

ELECTRICITY

The power supply in Britain is 240 volts. Sockets only accept three (square)-pin plugs, so an adaptor is needed for Continental and US

appliances. A transformer is needed for appliances operating on 110–120 volts.

CURRENCY AND FOREIGN EXCHANGE

Currency Britain's currency is the pound (£), issued in notes of £5, £10, £20 and £50. There are 100 pennies or pence (p) to each pound and coins come in denominations of 1p, 2p, 5p, 10p, 20p, 50p, £1 and £2. Travellers' cheques may be accepted by some hotels, shops and restaurants. Travellers'

cheques in pounds are the most convenient.

Exchange There are bureaux de change in most major streets in cities and towns, as well as at airports, rail stations and Underground stations in central London. Rates vary, and may be higher than at banks. Commission rates should be clearly displayed.

Credit cards These are accepted practically everywhere. They can also be used for drawing money at cashpoints (ATMs), where you pay a fixed withdrawal fee.

HEALTH AND SAFETY

Drugs/medication Prescription and non-prescription drugs and medicines are available from chemists/ pharmacies. Pharmacists can advise on medication for common ailments. Chemists operate a roster so there will

TIPS/GRATUITIES

Yes ✓   No ✗

Restaurants (if service not included)	✓	10–15%
Cafés/bars	✗	
Taxis	✓	10% or round up
Porters	✓	£1/bag
Chambermaids	✓	50p–£1 per day
Cloakroom attendants	✓	loose change
Hairdressers	✓	10%
Toilets	✗	

always be one that is open 24 hours; notices in all pharmacy windows give details.

Safe water Tap water is safe to drink. Mineral water is widely available but is often expensive, particularly in restaurants.

Personal safety The cities, towns and villages of England are all generally safe places to be. You will find the police force friendly, helpful and approachable. To minimise the risk of personal crime:
● Don't carry more cash than you need and use the hotel safe or deposit boxes for storing valuables
● Beware of pickpockets in markets and crowded places
● Don't walk alone in dark streets, alleyways or pedestrian underpasses

TOILETS

All cities and most towns have acceptable public toilets (lavatories), which are either free or require a small fee. In addition, department stores, large supermarkets and motorway service stations have free toilets. It is not acceptable for non-customers to walk in and use the facilities in pubs, cafés and restaurants.

CLOTHING SIZES

France	UK	Rest of Europe	USA	
46	36	46	36	
48	38	48	38	
50	40	50	40	
52	42	52	42	
54	44	54	44	Suits
56	46	56	46	
41	7	41	8	
42	7.5	42	8.5	
43	8.5	43	9.5	
44	9.5	44	10.5	
45	10.5	45	11.5	Shoes
46	11	46	12	
37	14.5	37	14.5	
38	15	38	15	
39/40	15.5	39/40	15.5	
41	16	41	16	
42	16.5	42	16.5	Shirts
43	17	43	17	
36	8	34	6	
38	10	36	8	
40	12	38	10	
42	14	40	12	
44	16	42	14	Dresses
46	18	44	16	
38	4.5	38	6	
38	5	38	6.5	
39	5.5	39	7	
39	6	39	7.5	
40	6.5	40	8	Shoes
41	7	41	8.5	

Best places to see

1 Bath

www.visitbath.co.uk

Bath is best known for its sweeping crescents of Georgian townhouses and the remains of its Roman baths, now restored, in the centre of the city.

The Romans built a temple to the local water goddess Sulis here, and the first Bath spa (Aqua Sulis) was founded. The remains of the **Roman Baths** are among the most important in Europe, and heavily visited, being in the centre of town. Little survives from the Saxon and medieval towns which followed, though they were obviously of some importance. Edgar was crowned first king of all England here in 973.

The abbey church, completed in 1499, stands across an enclosed square and contains some splendid vaulting. Aside from a heavily restored section of the old city walls, the rest of Bath is dominated by the changes wrought by leisure developers in the middle of the 18th century. Bath was then reinvented as the spa playground of the century's nouveaux riches. The Royal Crescent, Paragon, Circus and Lansdown Crescent were all magnificent streets built to accommodate the pleasure-seekers who came to Bath for the waters and the social scene. Walking is the best way to see the city, as the one-way traffic system can feel chaotic, but there are a number of open-top bus tours which take in the less accessible sights.

Other sights include the **Museum of Costume** (housed in the Assembly Rooms, Cross Bath, Queen Square and Victoria Park) and the **American Museum of Decorative Art** at Claverton Manor.

✚ 12Q 🛈 Abbey Chambers ☎ 0906 711 2000

Roman Baths Museum
✉ Pump Room, Abbey Church Yard ☎ 01225 477785
🕓 Mar–Jun, Sep–Oct daily 9–5; Jul, Aug 9–9; rest of year 9.30–4.30 ✋ Expensive

Museum of Costume
✉ Bennett Street ☎ 01225 477789 🕓 Mar–Nov daily 11–5; Nov–Mar daily 11–4 ✋ Moderate

American Museum of Decorative Art
✉ Claverton Manor ☎ 01225 460503;
www.americanmuseum.org 🕓 Mar–Nov Tue–Sun 12–5; 25 Nov–17 Dec Tue–Sun 12–5. Closed mid-Dec–Mar ✋ Moderate

2 Cotswolds

The warmth of the honey-coloured stone villages and the rich green landscape make the Cotswolds one of England's most beautiful areas.

The Cotswolds, a range of hills divided into two by the River Chum, represent the quintessential English landscape; rolling green hills, patchwork fields, and picturesque towns and villages. They form an Area of Outstanding Natural Beauty covering 790sq miles (2,038sq km), and spanning six counties from Bath in the south to Edge Hill in the north.

The great parish churches and inns demonstrate the prosperity of the area which began in the late Middle Ages. Sheep farming underpinned this wealth and made a huge impact on

the landscape as the Cotswolds became rich on wool and cloth. Chipping Camden, Northleach and Cirencester contain good examples of 'wool churches', heavily adorned with gargoyles.

The often overcrowded village of Broadway acts as a gateway to the region, with tourist shops and tearooms abounding. Bourton-on-the-Water is another tourist hotspot, with the River Windrush running pleasantly through its centre. Upper and Lower Slaughter attract visitors as much for their peculiar names as their chocolate-box looks. You can get a better feel for the Cotswolds' charm in less-visited gems such as Stanton, Snowshill or Bibury. Arlington Row, a delightful terrace of former weavers' cottages in Bibury best epitomizes Cotswold village character, and the nearby **Arlington Mill** houses an excellent folk museum.

✚ 12R 🛈 Contact local tourist information offices for specific details. Cheltenham office: ☎ 01242 522878; www.visitcheltenham.gov.uk

Arlington Mill Museum
☎ 01285 740368 🕐 Mar–Oct daily 10–6; Nov–Feb Mon–Fri 10–5, Sat–Sun 10–5.30
✋ Inexpensive

3 Exmoor

www.visit-exmoor.info

Sweeping heather moors are split by wooded valleys, or coombs, which tumble into the sea in this national park on the border of Somerset and Devon.

Within the 265sq miles (426.5sq km) of Exmoor lie extensive heath and grass moors, woodlands and plantations, a high moorland plateau and steep-sided valleys, cultivated farmland and rough grazing, as well as splendid sea cliffs – features that have an important influence on the way the area is run.

The national park borders the Bristol Channel and enjoys a refreshing maritime climate. It reaches its highest point on Dunkery Beacon, at 1,702ft (519m) with breathtaking views of the valleys of the Barle, the Exe and the East and West Lyn rivers.

At the northern edge of the park the twin towns of Lynton and Lynmouth are linked by a 19th-century water-powered cliff railway. The lower town, at the mouth of the two Lyn rivers, was

famously devastated by a flood in 1953. The upper town boasts fine views and leads to the spectacular, dry Valley of the Rocks, running parallel to the dramatic 500ft (150m) coastal cliffs. Nearby Watersmeet is a popular beauty spot deep in a tree-lined ravine where Hoar Oak Water joins the East Lyn River. This is superb walking country. For many people, however, Exmoor is synonymous with R D Blackmore's novel, *Lorna Doone*

NATIONAL PARK
EXMOOR

– a tale of thwarted love, villains and passion set amid the brooding moors, published in 1869. Henry Williamson's classic wildlife story, *Tarka the Otter*, was also inspired by the author's time at Exmoor. Among the wildlife found on Exmoor is the red deer, the stag's antlers making up the National Park logo.

🕂 10Q ✉ Exmoor National Park, Fore Street, Dulverton, Somerset TA22 9EX ☎ 01398 323665

4 Hadrian's Wall

www.hadrians-wall.org

The purpose of this great Roman wall was 'to separate the Romans from the Barbarians' – *'qui barbaros Romanosque divideret...'*

One of a series of Roman boundary fortifications built right across northern Europe, Hadrian's Wall stretches for 73 miles (117km) between Wallsend, on the east coast near Newcastle upon Tyne, to Bowness-on-Solway in Cumbria on the west coast. Begun in AD 122, the wall took six years to complete and is 10ft (3m) thick in places. The walkway which ran along the top was sometimes as high as 3.5m (12ft) above the ground.

The wall was built to protect Roman Britain from raiding Picts from what is now Scotland, and the most dramatic sections still run close to the Anglo-Scottish border. Hadrian's wall was abandoned in AD 383, much of the stone from the wall was used in local buildings, but enough remains to give a vivid picture of a Roman frontier province. A World Heritage Site, there are many museums and interpretive centres along the wall that portray life in Roman times, notably at Birdoswald, Once Brewed, Vindolanda and Chesters, but the best is the **Housesteads Fort and Museum.** Known to the Romans as Vercovicium, Housesteads is the most complete Roman fort in Britain, and occupies a spectacular position with commanding views across the bleak Northumbrian countryside. It was garrisoned by about 1,000 soldiers and the museum recreates aspects of their life as well as explaining the natural history of the region. Walkers can follow the course of the wall along a National Trail.

🚪 3K 🛈 The Manor Office, Hallgate, Hexham, Northumberland, NE46 1XD ☎ 01434 652220

Housesteads Fort and Museum

✉ Housesteads ☎ 01434 344363 🕐 Apr–Sep daily 10–6; Oct–Mar daily 10–4. Closed 24–26 Dec, 1 Jan 🖐 Moderate

5 Lake District

www.lake-district.gov.uk

Few places in England have the richly varied landscape of the Lake District; fewer still its wealth of local history and legends.

The Lake District, which forms part of Cumbria in northwest England, is acknowledged nationally and internationally as a special place of natural beauty, drawing visitors from all over the world. Covering 885sq miles (2,292sq km) this is the largest and most spectacular of England's national parks. It contains England's biggest lakes and mountains, in a combination that is never less than exhilarating. Windermere is England's longest lake (10.5 miles/ 17km from Waterhead to Lakeside), Wastwater its deepest (258ft/79m) and Scafell Pike its highest mountain at 3,210ft (978m).

The Lake District is basically a system of valleys (or 'dales') radiating from a central core of mountains, known as 'fells' (from the Norse settlers' 'fjall'). This is prime walking country and thousands flock to the popular summits, such as Scafell Pike, Helvellyn, Skiddaw and Great Gable. Despite their modest altitude, the weather can be very severe here and care should be taken. However, there are over 1,500 miles (2,414km) of footpaths covering all types of terrain, from lakesides to quiet forests and exhilarating open moors, ensuring a level of walking to suit everyone.

Of the principal tourist centres, Windermere (town), Bowness and Kendal attract thousands of daytrippers and are easily accessible by road and

rail. Many make for the **Visitor Centre** at Brockhole. Keswick, in the north, nestles amid towering fells beside Derwent Water and has a seemingly limitless development of outdoor clothing shops. Ambleside, at the head of Windermere (lake), in the south, plays a similar role. Grasmere, with nearby Rydal, is between the two and famously associated with the poet William Wordsworth, a Cumbrian who did much of his best work while living here.

To escape the crowds in this heavily visited region, you should make for the fringes of the national park. Wasdale and Eskdale in the west, and Mardale and Swindale in the east are quieter valleys without the occasional summer traffic problems which curse the centre of the park. But on most days, even the popular valleys of Langdale, Buttermere and Borrowdale are surprisingly peaceful.

✚ 1J
Lake District Visitor Centre
✉ Brockhole (on A591 between Windermere and Ambleside), Cumbria ☎ 01539 446601 🕐 Apr–Nov daily 10–5. Grounds and gardens: daily 🎟 Free; parking £4 per day

Oxford

www.visitoxford.org

Oxford is an important industrial and commercial centre, dominated both historically and physically by its university.

Modern Oxford sprawls eastwards and includes car plants and technology industries as well as the more predictable publishing houses and English language schools within its city limits. The University's 36 colleges are large and complex institutions and exert considerable influence, though they do not entirely monopolize city life.

It is the architecture of the colleges which first impresses the visitor. There are masterpieces from

many periods, from the early Gothic of Merton College to the experimental modernism of St Catherine's. The location of the college buildings in the heart of the city gives Oxford a truly historic feel. The parklands, preserved by the various colleges, that surround the centre and the various cyclists, punters and rowers, all add to the ambience of gentility. There has been educational influence in the city since at least 1167 when students expelled from Paris settled here under the patronage of Henry II. The colleges, with their quadrangles, refectories and chapels, still reflect the religious houses upon which they were founded.

Of outstanding interest is the **Ashmolean Museum,** England's oldest public museum, founded in 1683. It houses the University's enormous collections of art and antiquities. On the corner of Broad Street you'll also find the **Bodleian Library** and the Sheldonian Theatre.

✚ 14R 🛈 16 Broad Street ☎ 01865 726871 🕓 Mon–Sat 9.30–5, Sun 10–4

Ashmolean Museum
✉ Beaumont Street ☎ 01865 278000; www.ashmol.ox.ac.uk 🕓 Tue–Sat 10–5, Sun 12–5. Closed 1 Jan, Good Fri–Easter Sun, 3 days early Sep, 24–28 Dec ✋ Free ❓ Guided tours

Bodleian Library
✉ Broad Street ☎ 01865 277180; www.bodley.ox.ac.uk 🕓 Mon–Fri 9–5 (times may vary), Sat 9–1. Closed 25 Dec and Easter ✋ Inexpensive ❓ Guided tours: daily 10.30, 11.30, 2pm, 3pm

7 Stonehenge

www.english-heritage.org.uk/stonehenge

The great stone circle at Stonehenge is one of the wonders of the world, as old as many of the temples and pyramids of Egypt.

Stonehenge (from the Old English 'hanging stones') is 2 miles (3km) west of Amesbury in Wiltshire, and one of the best-known archaeological sites in the world. It is not, as might be supposed, an isolated monument. In reality, the stones are part of an extensive prehistoric landscape filled with the remains of ceremonial and domestic structures.

What you see today is the last in a series of monuments erected in several stages between 3000 and 1600BC. Each is circular in form and aligned along the rising of the sun at the midsummer solstice, though many of the structures are now incomplete.

Archaeologists still debate whether Stonehenge was a place of ritual sacrifice and sun worship, some kind of astronomical calculator, or a royal palace. But for thousands of years it was an important focal point within a ceremonial landscape. The structure also represents a massive investment in time and human resources. Enormous effort was needed to transport the stones, some weighing up to 40 tons, from sites tens or hundreds of miles away, notably from Preseli in Wales, from where they must have been dragged or floated on rafts.

Stonehenge is now a UNESCO World Heritage Site, and although conflict has arisen between modern druids, new-age travellers and the police over access to the site, there is no doubt that its conservation has been taken very seriously. There are recommended walks exploring the surrounding downland of Salisbury Plain and an archaeological leaflet available from the gift shop to help you interpret this ancient landscape.

✚ 13Q ✉ Near Amesbury, Wiltshire ☎ 0870 333 1181
🕐 Mid-Mar to Jun, Sep to mid-Oct daily 9.30–6; Jun–Sep daily 9–7; mid- to late Oct daily 9.30–5; late Oct to mid-Mar daily 9.30–4. Closed 24–26 Dec and 1 Jan 🖐 Moderate
🍴 Stonehenge Kitchen (£–££) ❓ Self-guided audio tours

8 Tower of London

www. hrp.org.uk

Overlooking the Thames, the Tower of London is famous as a place of imprisonment and death; it's also one of England's foremost medieval fortresses.

The Tower, not just one tower but a whole castle-full, is one of London's great landmarks. It has been

ENTRY TO THE TRAITORS GATE

a royal residence, an armoury and the home, as it still is, of the Crown Jewels. It is surrounded by Tower Green, where the executions of three of Henry VIII's wives (Lady Jane Grey, Anne Boleyn and Catherine Howard) took place. Here you'll find two of the Tower's famous ravens, the latest in a long line protected by royal decree. Their wings are clipped to stop them flying away, for should they leave, legend claims the Tower and kingdom will fall.

Walks around the Tower are conducted by Yeoman Warders (Beefeaters), who recount tales of torture and intrigue.

The Crown Jewels are housed in the Jewel House. Viewing them is a rather hurried affair as visitors are carried along moving walkways. Among the dazzling display is the Imperial State Crown which contains a 317-carat diamond, sapphires, emeralds, rubies and pearls, but the most famous of the diamonds is the Koh-i-Noor, set into a crown made for the Queen Mother in 1937.

In the Bloody Tower are the rooms where the 'Princes in the Tower', the 12-year-old Edward V and his brother Richard, were murdered by Richard III and where Sir Walter Raleigh was held captive for 13 years.

✠ *London 8e (off map)* ☎ 0870 756 6060 🕐 Mar–Oct Tue–Sat 9–6, Sun–Mon 10–6; Nov–Feb Tue–Sat 9–5, Sun–Mon 10–5. Last admission 1 hour before closing. Closed 1 Jan, 24–26 Dec 💷 Very expensive 🍴 Café (£) 🚇 Tower Hill 🚌 15, 25, 42, 78, 100, D1 🚉 Fenchurch Street (National Rail); Tower Gateway (DLR) ❓ Buy tickets in advance from any underground station to avoid waiting. Free hour-long tours run about every half hour

York

www.visityork.org

York is one of the few cities in England that still feels medieval. Begun by the Romans in AD 71, it became an important city, which they called Eboracum.

'York' comes from the Scandanavian *Jorvik*, and the **Viking Centre** in Coppergate houses a vivid display of York under Scandanavian domination. Later, the Normans made York their centre of government, commerce and religion in the north. Taking centre stage is the magnificent Minster, which took 250 years to build and was completed and consecrated in 1472. Now one of the city's essential visitor attractions, it contains England's finest collection of medieval stained glass.

During the Middle Ages, York was an important wool-trading centre. On the prosperity of this trade rode the success of other tradespeople, notably goldsmiths, butchers, shoemakers and saddlers, who came to live in the city. Many of these traders lived in Stonegate, Goodramgate and the Shambles, streets which are still very medieval in

appearance; the modern shops her are shaped around the plots laid out over 1,000 years ago.

The medieval city walls are also largely intact and make an interesting circular walk of around 2.5 miles (4km). Beyond the walls, the **National Railway Museum** is the keeper of Britain's railway heritage and is well worth visiting for its huge displays from the golden age of steam.

✚ 4G 🚹 St Leonard's Place, De Grey rooms YO1 7HB
☎ 01904 621756 🕓 Mon–Sat 9–6, Sun 10–5

Jorvik Viking Centre

✉ Coppergate ☎ 01904 643211; www.vikingjorvik.com
🕓 Apr–Oct daily 10–5; Nov–Mar daily 10–4 ✋ Moderate

National Railway Museum

✉ Leeman Road 🕓 Daily 10–6 ☎ 01904 321261;
www.arm.org.uk ✋ Moderate

10 Yorkshire Dales

www.yorkshiredales.co.uk

A series of charming upland valleys, each with a distinctive character, makes up this popular national park.

Lying astride the Pennines in the north of England, the Yorkshire Dales are a popular area of rugged moorlands, rivers, streams (here called becks and valleys – the 'dales'), patterned by hedgerows, drystone walls and villages. The principal dales – Airedale, Wharfedale, Nidderdale, Wensleydale and Swaledale – have a distinctive character and culture and noticeably different dialects. But the landscape unites them, with its open fells, heather moors, limestone crags and close-cropped turf.

The region is honeycombed with cave systems so complex that some remain unexplored. There are show caves at Clapham and near Grassington. Grassington itself, a delightful village around a small square in Wharfedale, has a fine museum of Dales life. Nearby Bolton Priory is a medieval abbey picturesquely situated in meadowland, surrounded by woods and rolling moorland. Airedale's biggest attraction is Malham Cove, a huge 250ft (76m) inland cliff which dominates the head of the valley. Wensleydale, famous for its cheese, lies further

north and boasts several spectacular waterfalls as well as the busy little market town of Hawes. Swaledale is altogether more remote and wild, its northern fringe sloping off into the high moorlands of the North Pennines. Lead mining was very important here until the end of the 19th century and the area's gills (side valleys) bear the healed scars of this industry.

The surrounding towns such as Settle and Ingleton in the west, Skipton (► 112–113) in the south and Richmond (► 110) and Leyburn in the east make excellent centres for exploration. This is splendid walking country, spanned by the Pennine Way National Trail and other recreational paths, and a challenge walk links the region's three highest peaks: Pen-y-Ghent, Whernside and Ingleborough.

✚ 3H ✉ Yorkshire Dales National Park Authority, Colvend, Hebden Road, Grassington, Skipton, West Yorkshire BD23 5LB ☎ 01756 751694; www.yorkshiredales.org.uk or www.yorkshirevisitor.com ⚙ Apr–Nov daily 10–5; Dec–Mar Sat–Sun only

Best things to do

Good places to have lunch

Antony's (££–£££)
Accolades have been heaped upon this father-and-son-run restaurant, which opened in 2004. The set lunch is a bargain introduction to their adventurous, world-class cooking.
✉ 19 Boar Lane, Leeds ☎ 0113 245 5922

Brown's (££)
Former corn mill on the banks of the River Severn, with cream walls and high ceilings. English food with a modern twist.
✉ South Quay, Worcester ☎ 01905 26263

The Glass House (£–££)
Restored mill building with huge windows. Contemporary Mediterranean dishes alongside traditional British food.
✉ Rydal Road (next to Adrian Sankey's glass-blowing shop), Ambleside, Cumbria ☎ 01539 432137

Green's Café (£)
A varied selection of sandwiches, paninis and good coffee is on the menu in Jan Rasmussen's welcoming café, but his secret weapon is free wi-fi for laptop users.
✉ 50 St.Giles, Oxford ☎ 01865 316878

The Jolly Sportsman (£–££)
Marvellous beers are served at this word-of-mouth gastropub and the food is equally enticing, with seafood a speciality.
✉ Chapel Lane, East Chiltington, East Sussex ☎ 01273 890400

The Old Success Inn (£–££)
A fishing inn dating from the 17th century, serving home-made specials, seafood and sandwiches.
✉ Sennen Cove, Cornwall ☎ 01736 871232

Pump Room (££)

Be serenaded by musicians as you have lunch or sip afternoon tea at this Georgian pump room.

✉ Abbey Church Yard, Bath ☎ 01225 444477

The Refectory (£)

Good coffee and light snacks served in the atmospheric cloisters.

✉ Cathedral Cloisters, Wells, Somerset

Tate Britain Restaurant (££)

Rex Whistler's murals here provide the backdrop to unfussy food.

✉ Millbank, London ☎ 020 7887 8000

Places to take the children

Eureka

Award-winning hands-on museum of science designed especially
for children.

✉ Discovery Road, Halifax, West Yorkshire ☎ 01422 330069;
www.eureka.org.uk ⚙ Daily 10–5; closed 24–26 Dec ✋ Moderate

Flambards Village

Family attraction including Victorian village, rides, aviation display,
science centre and wartime displays.

✉ Culdrose Manor, Helston, Cornwall ☎ 01326 573404;
www.flambards.co.uk ⚙ Apr–Oct daily 10.30–5; Nov–Mar daily 11–4
✋ Expensive (includes all rides and entertainment)

Ironbridge Gorge Museums

The world's first iron bridge was cast and built here in 1779. Now
the site of a splendid series of ten historical industrial museums
and exhibitions that are endlessly fascinating (➤ 124–125).

✉ Ironbridge, Telford, Shropshire ☎ 01952 884391; www.ironbridge.org.uk
⚙ Daily 10–5. Some museums closed Nov–Mar ✋ Moderate–expensive;
ask about a passport to all museums

Legoland Windsor

This gloriously landscaped theme park in miniature is dedicated
to the imagination and creativity of children. It was specifically
designed for the under-12s and will easily keep kids amused for
a day.

✉ Windsor Park, Windsor, Berkshire ☎ 0870 504 0404; www.legoland.co.uk
⚙ Mar–Oct daily 10–5 ✋ Very expensive

Madame Tussaud's

World leaders, musicians, athletes and film actors stand side by
side in this legendary exhibition of wax figures in London.

✉ Marylebone Road ☎ 0870 400 3000; www.madame-tussauds.co.uk
⚙ Mon–Fri 9.30–5.30, Sat–Sun 9–6 ✋ Very expensive 🚇 Baker Street

Magna

Science adventure centre exploring earth, air, fire, water and power with lots of hands-on, interactive challenges. There are five adventure pavilions, two shows and an outdoor adventure park.

✉ Sheffield Road, Templeborough, Rotherham ☎ 01709 720002; www.visitmagna.co.uk ⏰ Daily 10–5; closed 24–25 Dec ✋ Moderate

National Maritime Museum

Britain's seafaring history; the world of Nelson and the glory of the British Empire; 20th-century seapower and luxury liners.

✉ Romney Road, Greenwich, London ☎ 020 8858 4422, www.nmm.ac.uk ⏰ Daily 10–5 ✋ Free 🚇 DLR: Cutty Sark

Norfolk Broads Wildlife Centre and Country Park

A large collection of British and European wildlife set in parkland, with a pets' corner, play areas, model farm and trout pool.

✉ Great Witchingham, Norfolk ☎ 01952 884391; www.norfolkwildlife.co.uk ⏰ Apr–Oct daily 10–5 ✋ Moderate

Speedwell Cavern

Go down 105 steps to a boat that takes you more than a mile through underground, water-filled caverns.

✉ Winnats Pass, Castleton, Derbyshire ☎ 01433 620512; www.speedwellcavern.co.uk ⏰ Mon–Fri 10–5, Sat–Sun 10–5.30 ✋ Moderate

Good pubs

The Britannia Inn

Everything you would expect from a traditional British inn. The Britannia stands next to a village green shared with an ancient maple tree.

✉ Elterwater, Cumbria ☎ 01539 437210

Cott Inn

A warm, friendly pub with open fires, flagstones and brasses.

✉ Cott, Dartington, Devon ☎ 01803 863777

The George Inn

A truly traditional Dales pub with plenty of character – white-washed walls, stone-flaggged floor, beamed ceilings, open fires and 18th-century charm.

✉ Hubberholme, Wharfedale, North Yorkshire ☎ 01756 760808

The George of Stamford

A smart and busy old coaching inn built in 1597 for Lord Burghley, who was a statesman and an advisor to Queen Elizabeth I.

✉ 71 St Martin's, Stamford, Lincolnshire ☎ 01780 750750

Harrow Inn

Tucked away down a sleepy lane, this excellent, unspoiled country pub has been run by the same family since 1929.

✉ Steep, Hampshire ☎ 01730 262685

The Lamb Inn

The unchanging character and atmosphere of this civilized 500-year-old Cotswold inn appeals to everyone. The menu features new and traditional dishes using quality local produce.

✉ Sheep Street, Burford, Oxfordshire ☎ 01993 823155

The New Inn

An early 17th-century ivy-covered stone pub that is becoming especially popular for its imaginative blackboard 'specials'.

✉ Yealand Conyers, Lancashire ☎ 01524 732938

The Ringlestone Inn

An atmospheric 17th-century ale house on the top of the North Downs beside the Pilgrims Way. The pies and speciality sausages are an established favourite among regulars.

✉ Ringlestone, Kent ☎ 01622 859900

The Saracen's Head

Out in the north Norfolk countryside amid open fields, this pub has a cosy parlour room with an open fire and a sheltered courtyard for summer dining. Originality and quality that count most and the menu features some local dishes and produce.

✉ Wolterton, Erpingham, Norfolk ☎ 01263 768909

Best houses and gardens

HOUSES
Audley End House
Fine Jacobean house with 30 rooms open to the public. Landscaped by Capability Brown.

✉ Saffron Walden, Suffolk ☎ 01799 522399 🕓 Grounds: Wed–Sun 10–6. House: Wed–Fri, Sat 11–2, Sun 11–4 ✋ Moderate

Hampton Court Palace
Splendid Tudor palace on the River Thames; for centuries the home of British monarchs.

✉ Hampton Court, Surrey ☎ 0870 7527777; www.hampton-court-palace.co.uk 🕓 Mar–Oct daily 10–6; Nov–Mar daily 10–4; times may vary ✋ Expensive

Hardwick Hall
Exceptional 16th-century house built for Bess of Hardwick with much of the original furnishings. Rare breeds in the huge park.

✉ Near Chesterfield, Derbyshire ☎ 01246 850430 🕓 Mar–Nov Wed–Thu, Sat–Sun 12–4.30; times may vary ✋ Moderate

Petworth House and Park
Unrivalled art collection, fine woodcarvings and a deer park.

✉ Petworth, Sussex ☎ 01798342207 🕓 Sat–Wed 11–5 ✋ Moderate (Park: free)

GARDENS
Clumber Park
Huge country park encompassing forest, parkland, a lake and a

walled kitchen garden. Special weekend events in summer.
✉ Worksop, Nottinghamshire ☎ 01909 476592 🕐 Daily dawn–dusk. Gardens: daily 10–5 ✋ Inexpensive

Harlow Carr Botanical Garden
The Royal Horticultural Society's show garden in the north, with ornamental and woodland areas.
✉ Cragg Lane, Harrogate, Yorkshire ☎ 01423 565418 🕐 Mar–Oct daily 9.30–5 ✋ Moderate

Lost Gardens of Heligan
Magnificent reclaimed gardens with a jungle garden, pineapples in heated glasshouses and a crystal grotto.
✉ Pentewan, St Austell, Cornwall ☎ 01726 845100; www.heligan.com 🕐 Mar–Oct daily 10–6; Nov–Mar 10–5 ✋ Moderate

Sheffield Park Garden
Landscaped by Capability Brown, with four large lakes, cascades, rhododendrons and azaleas.
✉ Sheffield Park, Sussex ☎ 01825 790231 🕐 Jun–Oct Tue–Sun 10.30–6 ✋ Moderate

Westonbirt Arboretum
One of Europe's largest collection of trees and shrubs. Glorious displays year-round.
✉ Near Tetbury, Gloucestershire ☎ 01666 880220 🕐 Daily 10–dusk ✋ Moderate

Top outdoor activities

Go to a football match. Although tickets may be hard to come by for the big-name teams, provincial town matches on a Saturday are no problem.

Go for a country walk in one of the national parks. Park information offices have leaflets about guided trails and wildlife.

Rent a boat and go rowing on a park lake or river. In Oxford or Cambridge, take out a punt, student-style.

Go horse riding. There are British Horse Society (BHS) approved riding schools in most areas. Tourist offices can supply details.

Walk a town trail – it's one of the best ways of getting to know a place: leaflets are usually available at the local tourist information centre.

Tour the country lanes on a rented bike – and take a picnic. Norfolk is one of England's flattest counties.

Have a flutter at a horse race. There are racecourses all over the country. For more information, visit www.bhb.co.uk

Watch one of the local cricket matches that are played around the country on Saturday afternoons during summer.

Try beachcombing, particularly out of season when much of the coastline is deserted.

Visit one of England's many ancient stone sites, such as Avebury in Wiltshire or Castlerigg in Cumbria.

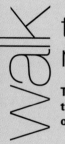

a walk

through London's royal parks

The royal parks are wonderful oases of green in the very heart of London; this walk links four of them.

Begin from Westminster, opposite the Houses of Parliament. Cross Parliament Square and go into Great George Street. Take the first right, and turn into St James's Park.

St James's is the oldest and most attractive of the central London parks, established by Henry VIII in the 1530s.

Keep to the left of the lake until you can cross it by a bridge.

The views from the bridge are splendid in both directions: face the impressive buildings of Whitehall, and behind you lies Buckingham Palace.

Over the bridge, turn left, and go up to join The Mall. Cross The Mall and walk towards Buckingham Palace. Keep right, by the edge of Green Park, and up Constitution Hill. Tackle the Green Park and Hyde Park Corner pedestrian underpass as if going to Hyde Park station, but continue instead up to the Park.

Hyde Park (► 81) originally belonged to the Church, until Henry VIII seized it to use as hunting grounds.

By keeping to the eastern side of the park you eventually find your way to Marble Arch. Go through the pedestrian underpass here, to exit 14 onto Oxford Street. Keep walking straight along Oxford Street until you can turn left onto Portman Street. Turn right into Portman Square and walk along until you reach the crossroads of Baker and Wigmore Street, turning left to walk along Baker Street and the another side of Portman Square. Continue along Baker Street for a short distance to reach Regent's Park. Return from Baker Street station.

Distance 4.25 miles (7km)
Time 3–4 hours including stops
Start point Houses of Parliament ➕ *London 4b*
End point Regent's Park ➕ Off map
Lunch Serpentine Cafe (£)

Ways to be a local

Have lunch at a country pub and try out the local ales while enjoying a traditional roast or ploughman's (a meal of bread, cheese or meat with pickle and salad).

Eat cake and sandwiches in the afternoon at a tea room or café.

Take a walk in the park. Practically every town has at least one.

Don't be put off by the weather forecast; always carry an umbrella; and dress in layers.

Enjoy a full English breakfast from a 'greasy spoon' cafe.

Be flexible – change your plans to suit your mood.

Visit a traditional seaside resort, such as Mablethorpe on the east coast or Margate in Kent.

Shop at a street market – these are excellent places to go bargain hunting.

Buy a large-scale road map and leave the main roads. You'll discover villages, farm shops, stately homes, gardens and quiet places to walk in the countryside.

Enjoy fish and chips from a corner chip shop or 'chippy'– every town has several, but they always taste best at the seaside.

Best places to stay

Bovey Castle Hotel (££–£££)

Luxury in the heart of Dartmoor: elegant bedrooms, ornate public rooms, a fine restaurant and championship golf course.
✉ Moretonhampstead, Devon ☎ 01647 440355

The Dorchester (£££)

World class; beautifully furnished bedrooms with sumptuous bathrooms – everything you would expect at this level of service.
✉ 53 Park Lane, London ☎ 020 7629 8888 Ⓜ Hyde Park Corner

The Feathers at Ludlow (££)

This historic, long-established hotel dates back to the 17th century and features exposed timbers, ornate ceilings and oak panelling. The spacious modern bedrooms are well-equipped.
✉ Bull Ring, Ludlow, Shropshire ☎ 01584 875261

Gravetye Manor (£££)

A stone-built Elizabethan mansion, standing at the end of a long drive through Forestry Commission land; the interior is characterized by highly polished wooden surfaces, open log fires, floral displays and spacious bedrooms with comfortable furniture and modern amenities.

✉ Vowles Lane, East Grinstead, West Sussex ☎ 01342 810567

Le Manoir aux Quat'Saisons (£££)

The lovely gardens around this 15th-century manor house supply the vegetables and herbs for the hotel's highly respected kitchens; an outstanding hotel and restaurant patronized by French chef Raymond Blanc.

✉ Church Road, Great Milton, Oxfordshire ☎ 01844 278881

Le Meridien Victoria and Albert (££–£££)

Imaginatively created from old warehouses, this modern hotel stands on the banks of the River Irwell and provides easy access to Manchester's heritage and shopping sites; excellent restaurant.

✉ Water Street, Manchester ☎ 0161 832 1188

Le Meridien York (££–£££)

Reminiscent of an age of past elegance, this magnificent, refurbished and restored Victorian hotel offers a pleasing atmosphere of romantic splendour and is set within its own private grounds overlooking the city walls.

✉ Station Road, York ☎ 01904 653681

Exploring

Small as England may look on the map, it is packed with things to see and do and the landscape and architecture can change within a few miles. Between London – one of the great capital cities of the world – to the myriad tiny villages with little more than a church and a few houses – you'll find splendid stately homes, pretty market towns, ancient monuments, fabulous gardens, as well as internationally renowned art, history and retail therapy.

In the north are the mountains of the Lake District and the huge open spaces of Northumbria; Yorkshire and the Peak District below offer moorland and dales. In the south the coastline of the West Country contrasts with the heaths and orchards of the more populated southeast. In between are the Cotswolds, dotted with picture-perfect stone villages and the fenlands of East Anglia with their magical waterways.

London

London is one of Europe's biggest cities, with a population of over 7 million and an area spreading for more than 620sq miles (992sq km) from its heart along the River Thames. It is a place with unequalled charisma and an almost tangible air of constant excitement that comes as much from the amazingly cosmopolitan make-up of its resident population as from the 'buzz' of a capital city.

Yet, in spite of the constant activity, there are many oases of peace and quiet. London's public parks, gardens, museums and historic churches rival the best in the world – many of them tucked away from the traffic congestion and the brouhaha of everyday life. Shopaholics will be in some kind of heaven here, whether rubbing shoulders with the high and mighty in Harrods or, at the other extreme, bustling with the hoi polloi at one of the many weekend street markets.

BRITISH MUSEUM

The British Museum, the world's first public museum, was created in 1753, following the death of Sir Hans Sloane, whose collection of over 80,000 artefacts was sold to the British government. The museum, the largest in the UK, moved to its present site in 1823 and contains over 6 million items. Worth singling out are the Elgin Marbles, the Rosetta Stone, the Oriental Collection, the Mexican Gallery and the Lindisfarne Gospels.

www.thebritishmuseum.ac.uk
✚ *London 4f* ✉ Great Russell Street, Bloomsbury ☎ 020 7636 1555, 020 7323 8000
🕐 Sat–Wed 10–5.30, Thu, Fri 10–8.30. Closed 1 Jan, Good Friday, 24–26 Dec. ✋ Free 🍴 Café (£); restaurant (££) Ⓜ Holborn, Tottenham Court Road, Russell Square

BUCKINGHAM PALACE

Built on the site of a brothel in 1703 to provide the Duke of Buckingham with a city residence, the palace, which was renovated during the 19th century, has served as the monarch's permanent London home since the time of Victoria. Eighteen of the 600 rooms are open to visitors for two months of the year; queues at the ticket office opposite in Green Park can be

considerable. The Changing of the Guard, which takes place daily at around 11.30, from April to July and on alternate days the rest of the year, doesn't involve queuing, and is the most popular reason for visiting the palace.

www.royalcollection.org.uk

➕ *London 2c* ✉ The Mall ☎ 020 7766 7300 ⏰ Aug and Sep daily 9.45–6, last admission 3.45 🎫 Very expensive Ⓖ Green Park, Hyde Park Corner, St James's Park, Victoria

COVENT GARDEN

Taking its name from a medieval convent garden, the bustling, pedestrianized piazza of Covent Garden was laid out by Inigo Jones in 1631, and was initially a very fashionable address. Forty years later, it had developed into the main London fruit and vegetable market, and became a notorious red-light district. In the 1830s the area was cleaned up and the splendid iron and glass hall you see today was built to house the market, which it did until this moved south of the river to Vauxhall in 1974. Today only some arcading and St Paul's Church remain of the original piazza. Street musicians and entertainers are a daily sight. The Royal Opera House (▶ 96) reopened in 1999 after a major refurbishment.

➕ *London 5e* 🍴 Numerous (£–££) Ⓖ Covent Garden

DOCKLANDS

Containerization brought the decline of London's enormous dockland area. For 20 years this part of the city lay derelict, until the 1980s when a development corporation was established to provide residential and office accommodation. The centrepiece is the Canary Wharf tower, at 800ft (244m), Britain's tallest building, designed by Cesar Pelli. The area is connected to central London by the Docklands Light Railway (DLR), with its distinctive driverless trains and the Jubilee line, whose Canary Wharf station was designed by Sir Norman Foster.

✚ *London 8e (off map)*

GREENWICH

Steeped in royal and naval history, Greenwich (pronounced Gren-itch), boasts some of London's finest architecture in the Royal Observatory, the Old Royal Naval College, Queen's House (a miniature palace built for the wife of James I) and the National Maritime Museum. The *Cutty Sark* is docked here on the Thames and Greenwich Park is one of the city's most attractive near by. Greenwich is also the site of the Greenwich Meridian.

✚ *London 8d (off map)* DLR Cutty Sark

HYDE PARK

Hyde Park is the largest and most famous of the central London parks. If you enter at Hyde Park Corner, you pass through Constitution Arch, commemorating Wellington's victory at Waterloo. Approach from Oxford Street, and you'll pass Marble Arch, designed by Nash in 1827 to imitate the Arch of Constantine in Rome; until 1851 it stood in front of Buckingham Palace (➤ 78–79). Near Marble Arch is Speaker's Corner, a platform for cranks, hecklers and religious extremists, and an ideal place for a little light entertainment. The **Serpentine Gallery,** to the west of the Serpentine lake, contains contemporary art exhibitions.

✚ *London 1c (off map)* 🍴 The Lido café (£) 🚇 Several including Marble Arch, Hyde Park Corner

Serpentine Gallery
☎ 020 7402 6075; www.serpetinegallery.org
🕓 Daily 10–6 during exhibitions
♿ Free 🚇 Lancaster Gate, South Kensington

LONDON EYE (BRITISH AIRWAYS)

Take a fun 30-minute ride on the world's largest observation wheel, erected for the millennium. An instantly recognizable addition to London's skyline, on a clear day you can see 25 miles (40km) out over the city. It is essential to buy tickets in advance to avoid waiting.

www.ba-londoneye.com

✚ *London 5c* ✉ Jubilee Gardens, South Bank ☎ 0870 5000 600, 0870 9908883 🎟 Expensive 🚇 Waterloo

MUSEUM OF LONDON

Beginning with a Prehistoric Gallery, then progressing chronologically, the Museum of London tells the story of the history of the capital. Very few of London's ancient buildings remain, but since World War II many important Roman, Saxon and Tudor discoveries have been made and are on display here. You will also find the Lord Mayor's Coach, a replica of a Newgate prison cell and the story of the Great Fire of London.

www.museumoflondon.org.uk

✚ *London 8f* ✉ London Wall ☎ 0870 444 3852 🎟 Free 🍴 Millburn Restaurant (£) 🚇 Barbican, Moorgate

NATIONAL GALLERY

Housing over 2,000 paintings, and taking up the whole of the north side of Trafalgar Square, the National Gallery contains one of the finest and most comprehensive collections of Western art in the world. The collection is divided chronologically, beginning with medieval and early Renaissance work, and includes *The Virgin of the Rocks* by Leonardo da Vinci, *Venus and Mars* by Botticelli, *Doge Leonardo Loredan* by Giovanni Bellini and *The Battle of San Romano* by Uccello. Because of the sheer scale of the place, it's a good idea to stop by the Micro Gallery, where, with the aid of computers, you can plan your own tour.

www.nationalgallery.org.uk

🚩 *London 4d* 🖂 Trafalgar Square ☎ 020 7747 2885 🕐 Mon–Sun 10–6, Wed 10–9. Closed 1 Jan, 24–26 Dec 🖐 Free 🍴 Café (£), Brasserie (££) Ⓜ Charing Cross

NATURAL HISTORY MUSEUM

The museum building, constructed in neo-Gothic cathedral style in the 1870s, impresses as much as the exhibits. No visit to the Museum would be complete without seeing the dinosaurs, and (unless you're squeamish about these things) the Creepy Crawlies exhibition – a great favourite with children. This is a far cry from the traditional image of a natural history museum, combining a wealth of content with imaginative new technology.

www.nhm.ac.uk

🚇 *London 1c (off map)* ✉ Cromwell Road and Exhibition Road ☎ 020 7942 5000 🕐 Mon–Sat 10–5.50, Sun 11.50 👤 Free Ⓜ South Kensington

PALACE OF WESTMINSTER

Parliament has not always met in London, but the first Palace of Westminster was built here around 1050 by Edward the Confessor, and significantly extended by William the Conqueror. There are two debating chambers, the House of Commons and the House of Lords. You can wait for a seat in the Visitors' Gallery on 'sitting days', normally Monday, Tuesday and Thursday afternoons for the Commons and Monday to Thursday afternoons for the Lords, by waiting outside St Stephen's entrance.

The building's best-known feature is the clock tower, Big Ben, though this is more correctly the name for its 13.4 ton (13.7 tonne) bell, cast at the Whitechapel Bell Foundry in 1858 and named after Benjamin Hall, First Commissioner of Works at the time.

www.parliament.uk

🚩 *London 4b* ✉ St Margaret Street (public entrance) ☎ Commons: 020 7219 4272; Lords: 020 7219 3107 🖐 Free 🚇 Westminster

ROYAL BOTANIC GARDENS, KEW

Containing an outstanding collection of plants, trees and flowers from all parts of the world, Kew Gardens owe their origin to Augusta, the Dowager Princess of Wales and mother of George III. In 1759, she turned part of her estate into a botanical garden, primarily for educational and scientific purposes. By 1841, however, the garden had seriously declined and was handed over to the State. The following year, Sir William Hooker was appointed director and the gardens began to acquire their worldwide reputation.

www.kew.org

🚩 15Q ✉ Kew, Richmond ☎ 020 8332 5655 🕔 Apr–Aug Mon–Fri 9.30–6, Sat–Sun 9.30–7; Sep–Oct daily 9.30–5.30; Nov–Jan 9.30–3.45, Feb–Mar 9.30–5 🖐 Moderate 🍴 The Orangery (£–££) 🚇 Kew Gardens

ST PAUL'S CATHEDRAL

When Sir Christopher Wren completed St Paul's in 1711 it was hailed as the world's first Protestant cathedral. Work began after the Great Fire of London in 1666 had destroyed the previous cathedral. It continues to dominate the London skyline, towering above many newer buildings. Inside are Flaxman's Nelson Memorial and Steven's Duke of Wellington Monument, as well as the celebrated Whispering Gallery, with its eerie acoustic effects. Continue to the Golden Gallery for one of the finest views over the city of London.

✚ *London 8e* ✉ St Paul's Churchyard ☎ 020 7236 4128 🕐 Mon–Sat 8.30–4 ♿ Moderate 🍴 The Crypt Café (£), The Refectory Restaurant (£–££) Ⓣ St Paul's ❓ Tours available

SCIENCE MUSEUM

One of the world's finest collections of landmarks in industrial history, technological milestones, and truly fascinating objects, the Science Museum gives a wonderful exposition of how things work and how technology has developed. There are 40 galleries;

exhibits you wouldn't want to miss include the *Apollo 10* command module, Stephenson's *Rocket*, the prototype computer and the first iron lung. The museum is renowned for its pioneering interactive hands-on displays (there are over 2,000 of them) that make any visit a memorable experience.

☩ *London 1c (off map)* ✉ Exhibition Road, South Kensington ☎ 0870 870 4868 ⏰ Daily 10–6 💷 Free; charge for some individual attractions 🍴 Museum cafés (£), restaurant (£–££) 🚇 South Kensington

TATE BRITAIN

Tate Britain houses the national collection of British art from 1500 to the present, including the highlight, the Turner Bequest, as well as pre-Raphaelite works. Until 2000, the international modern art collection was housed here as well but these works now reside in the Tate Modern on Bankside (▶ 88).

www.tate.org.uk/britain

☩ *London 4a* ✉ Millbank ☎ 020 7887 8000; recorded information 020 7887 8008 ⏰ Daily 10–5.50 💷 Free (charge for some exhibitions) 🚇 Pimlico

TATE MODERN

Britain's national
collection of
international modern art
from 1900 to the
present day. The most
influential artists of the
20th century are
represented, including
Picasso, Matisse, Dalí,
Rodin, Gabo and Warhol.
✚ London 8d ✉ Bankside
☎ 020 7887 8888; recorded
information 020 7887 8008
🕓 Sun–Thu 10–6, Fri, Sat
10–10 💷 Free (charge for
some exhibitions)
🚇 Blackfriars, Southwark

TOWER OF LONDON

See pages 50–51.

TRAFALGAR SQUARE

The heart of London,
from where all road
distances are measured,
Trafalgar Square was
designed by John Nash in the 1830s, and built in honour of Lord
Nelson following his victory at the Battle of Trafalgar in 1805. The
square's centrepiece is Nelson's Column, 187ft (57m) high,
erected between 1839 and 1842.

Close by is the **Church of St Martin-in-the-Fields,** an attractive
building, famous for its classical music concerts and its social care

unit. There is an art gallery in the crypt, and a daily clothes and crafts market is held outside in the church grounds.

✝ *London 4d*

Church of St Martin-in-the-Fields

✉ Trafalgar Square ☎ Concert tickets: 020 7839 8362; general information: 020 7766 1100 ✋ Free 🍴 Café-in-the-Crypt (£) Ⓔ Charing Cross

VICTORIA AND ALBERT MUSEUM (V&A)

Originally called the South Kensington Museum, the V&A is dedicated to the applied arts, and was established to house the contents of the Great Exhibition of 1851. Today the museum displays cultural artefacts from around the world, especially from the Far East, and houses one of the world's finest collection of decorative arts. Some 8 miles (13km) and four storeys of corridors and rooms make it essential to obtain a map and index before setting off into the museum.

www.vam.ac.uk

➕ *London 1c (off map)* ✉ Cromwell Road, South Kensington ☎ 020 7942 2000; 🕒 Daily 10–5.45 (Wed until 10). Closed 24–26 Dec 🖐 Free 🍴 Café Espresso (£), The New Restaurant (£–££) 🚇 South Kensington

WESTMINSTER ABBEY

Dating from the 13th and 16th centuries, Westminster Abbey stands on the site of a Benedictine monastery which Edward the Confessor (reigned 1042–66) sought to enlarge, close to his Palace of Westminster (➤ 85). The abbey has been the setting for the coronation of every British monarch, except Edward V and Edward VIII, since the time of William the Conqueror. Today it is still a church, in use for regular worship, and over 3,000 people, including royalty, are either buried or memorialized here. The best monuments lie beyond the choir-screen, to see these you have to pay an admission charge.

www.westminster-abbey.org

➕ *London 4b* ✉ Parliament Square ☎ 020 7222 5152 🕒 Mon–Fri 9.30–3.45 and Wed 6–7, Sat 9.30–1.45. Closed Sun. (Times may vary) 🖐 Moderate (half price Wed evening) 🍴 Coffee stands only 🚇 Westminster, St James's Park

HOTELS

Athenaeum (£££)

This elegant hotel overlooking Green Park remains one of the most popular and friendly in London. Lovely bedrooms and a spa.

✉ 116 Piccadilly ☎ 020 7499 3464 🚇 Green Park

Avonmore Hotel (££)

A privately owned, award-winning B&B with just nine bedrooms and a friendly atmosphere.

✉ 66 Avonmore Road, Kensington ☎ 020 7603 3121 🚇 West Kensington

The Dorchester (£££)

See page 72.

Foreign Missions Club (£)

With only gentle emphasis on the religious atmosphere, this converted row of terrace houses offers unexpected peace and quiet and a very friendly atmosphere, at an exceptionally low price.

✉ 20–26 Aberdeen Park, Highbury ☎ 020 7226 2663 🚇 Highbury and Islington (10-minute walk)

London County Hall Travel Inn (££)

A large city-centre hotel that offers smart, spacious and well-equipped bedrooms, and is ideal for families.

✉ Belvedere Road ☎ 0870 238 3300 🚇 Waterloo

Mitre House Hotel (££)

A long-established, family-run hotel with good facilities, close to Hyde Park.

✉ 178–184 Sussex Gardens ☎ 020 7723 8040 🚇 Lancaster Gate

Swiss House Hotel (££)

Comfortable, well-situated 16-room hotel in a pretty residential area of South Kensington, convenient for museums and shopping.

✉ 171 Old Brompton Road, South Kensington ☎ 020 7373 2769 🚇 South Kensington, Gloucester Road

Thistle Tower (££)

A great location next to the Tower of London; large and modern.

✉ St Katharine's Way ☎ 020 7481 2575 🚇 Tower Hill

RESTAURANTS

Alastair Little Soho (£££)

Distinctive, stylish décor and light modern-European cooking are the hallmark here; reserve well in advance.

✉ 49 Frith Street, Soho ☎ 020 7734 5183 🕐 Mon–Fri 12–3, Mon–Sat 6–11.30 🚇 Leicester Square, Tottenham Court Road

Blues Bistro and Bar (£–££)

A trendy but not too trendy bistro and bar with a small and pleasant dining room serving American and European food at resasonable prices.

✉ 42–43 Dean Street 🕐 Mon–Fri lunch, dinner, Sat–Sun dinner only 🚇 Piccadilly Circus

Café-in-the-Crypt (£)

This tranquil oasis in the very heart of London lies beneath the Church of St-Martin-in-the-Fields on the edge of Trafalgar Square. Good salads, soups, sandwiches and light meals.

✉ Duncannon Street, Trafalgar Square 🕐 Sun–Wed 10–8 , Thu–Sat 10–11 🚇 Charing Cross, Leicester Square

Chez Gérard at the Opera Terrace (££)

A glass conservatory on top of Covent Garden's market provides a completely different atmosphere. Great place for steak and chips.

✉ First Floor, Opera Terrace, Covent Garden Central Market ☎ 020 7379 0666 🕐 Mon–Sun 12–11.30 🚇 Covent Garden

Gay Hussar (££)

London's favourite Eastern European restaurant serving good value Hungarian food. A favourite haunt of literary, musical and Bohemian types.

✉ 2 Greek Street ☎ 020 7437 0973 🕐 Lunch and dinner Mon–Sat 🚇 Tottenham Court Road

Gordon Ramsay (£££)

One of London's finest restaurants run by the celebrity chef. Excellent cuisine, prepared with imagination and flair. Reservations are essential, but only are only taken up to a month in advance.
✉ 68 Royal Hospital Road ☎ 020 7352 4441 🕐 Mon–Fri lunch, dinner
Ⓜ Sloane Square

River Café (£££)

Famous advocates of regional Italian cooking, the River Café set new standards with familiar Italian ingredients.
✉ Thames Wharf Studios, Rainville Road ☎ 020 7386 4200 🕐 Mon–Sat lunch, dinner, Sun lunch Ⓜ Hammersmith

Rock and Sole Plaice (£)

This long-established 'chippie' is ideal for a late evening snack if you're in the Covent Garden area.
✉ 47 Endell Street ☎ 020 7836 3785 🕐 Mon–Sat 11.30–11.30, Sun until 10 or 11 Ⓜ Covent Garden

Rules (£££)

London's oldest restaurant, opened in 1798 and was patronized by the likes of Charles Dickens, and Edward VII and Lillie Langtry. Serves top-quality British food and was inner of the 'Best British Food Award' 2003.
✉ 35 Maiden Lane, Covent Garden ☎ 020 7836 5314 🕐 Daily 12–12
Ⓜ Covent Garden

Soho Spice (££)

Probably the best value of all the Indian restaurants in Soho. Has a limited menu but the quality is very high.
✉ 124–126 Wardour Street ☎ 020 7434 0808 🕐 Mon–Sat 11.30–11.30, Sun 12–10.30 Ⓜ Leicester Square, Tottenham Court Road

SHOPPING

Bond Street

London's most exclusive shopping street is expensive for buying, but a great place for just looking. *Haute couture*, antiques, auction houses, fine-art galleries and jewellers predominate.

Ⓤ Green Park, Bond Street

Covent Garden

Head to Neal Street for specialty stores or stay in the piazza for small, individual shops in a buzzing traffic-free environment.

Ⓤ Covent Garden

Kensington

Inexpensive and retro clothing can be found at Kensington Market, while antiques and art abound on up-market Kensington High Street.

Ⓤ High Street Kensington

Kings Road

Birthplace of the mini-skirt and the Punk movement, the Kings Road is still up-to-the-minute on street fashion.

Ⓤ Sloane Square

Oxford Street

London's most frenetic shopping street presents a cacophony of global styles and noise and is good for chain shops and department stores.

Ⓤ Marble Arch, Bond Street, Oxford Circus, Tottenham Court Road

Regent Street

A handsome boulevard with many exclusive shops including gold, silver and jewellery at Mappin & Webb and Garrard & Co; toys at Hamleys, and an emporium at Liberty and a huge Apple store with all the latest gadgets

Ⓤ Oxford Circus, Piccadilly Circus

ENTERTAINMENT

ARTS AND CULTURE

London boasts many long-running shows, mainly in the West End, as well as mainstream theatres presenting Shakespeare and contemporary playwrights.

Barbican Centre

Europe's largest arts centre is the base for the London Symphony and English Chamber orchestras. Also houses art galleries and cinemas.

✉ Silk Street, EC2 ☎ 020 7628 2326; www.barbican.org.uk Ⓤ Barbican, Moorgate

Royal Opera House

Home of the Royal Ballet and the Royal Opera. Free lunchtime concerts and events in the new Linbury Studio Theatre.

✉ Bow Street, Covent Garden ☎ 020 7304 4000; www.royaloperahouse.org Ⓤ Covent Garden, Embankment

Sadler's Wells Theatre

Sadler's Wells is the centre of British contemporary dance as well as hosting touring companies.

✉ Rosebery Avenue ☎ 020 7863 8000; www.sadlerswells.com Ⓤ Angel

LIVE MUSIC AND COMEDY

The 100 Club

Originally just a jazz haunt, now soul, funk, swing and Latin sounds can be heard in this renowned subterranean club.

✉ 100 Oxford Street ☎ 020 7636 0933 Ⓤ Oxford Circus

The Jazz Café

Live jazz, as well as soul, world music and R&B.

✉ 5 Parkway, Camden Town ☎ 020 7916 6060 Ⓤ Camden Town

Ronnie Scott's

Long-established jazz club attracting the top names.

✉ 47 Frith Street ☎ 020 7439 0947 Ⓤ Leicester Square

Royal Albert Hall

Famous domed building staging major concerts, including classical music. The venue for the annual Proms (promenade concerts).

✉ Kensington Gore, Knightsbridge ☎ 020 7589 8212 Ⓤ South Kensington

Northern England

For so long tarred (unjustly) with the dark brush of industrial grime and deprivation, the North of England has done much to clean up its image, where cleaning up was needed. But so many parts of the northern counties have always been arbours of beautiful landscape and rural retreats to rival any in England.

The attractions of the Lake District, the Yorkshire Dales, the North York Moors and Northumberland have long been popular and are well known. Perhaps less renowned are the pretty villages and hamlets of

Lancashire and Durham and the quiet backwaters of delectable Calderdale. Today bright, bustling and thriving cities – Leeds, Manchester, Liverpool, Sheffield and many more – play a fundamental role in the tourism and leisure industry, enabling visitors to get the best out of their stay in the North.

ALNWICK CASTLE

The 11th-century Alnwick Castle came into the Percy family in 1309, and is the birthplace of Harry Hotspur (1364–1403), who was immortilized in Shakepeare's *Henry IV Part One*. Following the revolt against Henry IV and the Battle of Shrewsbury, where Hotspur was killed, the estates were temporarily confiscated. The Duke of Northumberland still lives here, in what is the second largest inhabited castle in England. The magnificent state rooms are furnished in Italian Renaissance style.

www.alnwickcastle.com

✚ 3L ☎ 01665 511100 🕒 Apr–Nov daily 10–6 ✋ Moderate 🍴 Castle tea room (£)

BERWICK-UPON-TWEED

England's most northerly town changed hands 14 times during the turbulent period when the English and Scots fought to control the borderlands. The town's 16th-century fortifications form the basis of the massively thick Elizabethan walls encircling the town, which took 11 years to complete. The town has three distinctive bridges: the Royal Border Railway Bridge, built after the style of a Roman aqueduct by Robert Stephenson in the 1840s, contrasts remarkably with the rather modest 15-arch Berwick Bridge, completed in 1624, and the poor, concrete offering of the 1920s' Royal Tweed Bridge. In the centre of town the old jail houses the **Cell Block Museum,** which depicts tales of crime and punishment.

✚ 3M 🚹 106 Marygate ✉ 01289 330733

Cell Block Museum

✉ Guildhall, Marygate ☎ 01289 330900 🕓 Easter–Sep Mon–Fri
✋ Inexpensive

CARLISLE

Carlisle is a border city, with a wide pedestrianized marketplace at its heart. Its name is derived from the Celtic word *caer* meaning fort. Scottish and English names and accents still mingle freely in its covered market and malls, though there is little today to hint at the troubles the city has faced. It was last besieged in 1745 by Bonnie Prince Charlie's Jacobite army. Chief among the city's

assets are the castle, the striking red sandstone cathedral, and the **Tullie House Museum and Art Gallery,** which dramatically portrays much of the city's turbulent past, as a Roman frontier settlement and as a border town. Carlisle is also the terminus for the scenic Settle–Carlisle railway.

www.historic-carlisle.org.uk

✚ 2K 🚹 Old Town Hall ☎ 01228 625600;

Tullie House Museum and Art Gallery

✉ Castle Street ☎ 01228 534781;
www.tulliehouse.co.uk 🕓 Nov–Mar Mon–Sat 10–4, Sun 12–4; Apr–Jun, Sep–Oct Mon–Sat 10–5, Sun 12–5; Jul–Aug Mon–Sat 10–5, Sun 11–5
✋ Moderate 🍴 The Garden Restaurant (£–££)

CASTLE HOWARD

The splendour of the 18th-century Castle Howard, near Malton, northeast of York, provided the setting for the television adaptation of Evelyn Waugh's *Brideshead Revisited*. There are richly furnished rooms and an outstanding estate to explore.
www.castlehoward.co.uk

✚ 4H ☎ 01653 648444 ⏱ House: Mar–Nov daily 11–4. Garden and shops: daily 10–4.30 ✋ Moderate 🍴 Cafe (£–££)

EDEN VALLEY

The River Eden flows down from the Pennine Fells through the market towns of Kirkby Stephen and Appleby-in-Westmorland before heading for the Solway Firth. Appleby is a pretty town of sandstone buildings, notably along its main street, with **Appleby Castle** at the top and St Lawrence's Church at the bottom.

✚ 2J

Appleby Castle

⏱ For opening times contact Appleby-in-Westmorland tourist information centre: 01768 351177 ✋ Moderate 🍴 The Castle Tea Shoppe (£)

FOUNTAINS ABBEY

In 1132 13 monks, rebelling against the relaxed order of their parent house, came to Fountains to begin an austere and simple life. When the Dissolution of the Monasteries brought abbey life to an end in the 16th century, they left behind the most complete Cistercian abbey remains in Britain. Too remote to be turned into a country house or plundered for building stone, the remains evoke the spirit of the religious community that lived here for 400 years. The Studley Royal Water Garden nearby is a spectacular garden and, with the abbey, has been designated a World Heritage Site.
www.fountainsabbey.org.uk

✚ 3H ✉ Studley Park, Fountains, Ripon ☎ 01765 608888 ⏱ Nov–Feb daily 10–4; Mar–Oct daily 10–5. Closed Fri Nov–Feb ✋ Moderate 🍴 Restaurant (£–££)

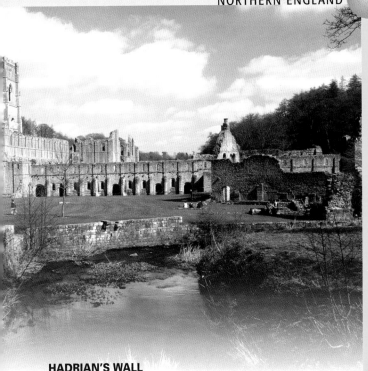

HADRIAN'S WALL

See pages 42–43.

HAWKSHEAD

Before the 19th century Hawkshead could not be reached by road, and the narrow streets in the village centre are still inaccessible by car. Wordsworth attended the grammar school here, which is now a museum and library. Beatrix Potter's husband, William Heelis, was a local solicitor, and his offices now house the **Beatrix Potter Gallery,** which contains original drawings from her books and tells the story of her life.

🚩 1J 🅸 Market Cross, Ambleside ☎ 01539 432582

Beatrix Potter Gallery

✉ Main Street, Hawkshead ☎ 01539 436355 🕔 Telephone for details, times vary 🖐 Inexpensive 🍴 Several in village (£–££)

HAWORTH

On the edge of the Pennine Moors, Haworth, scarcely less a literary shrine than Stratford-upon-Avon, is an attractive and busy little town famed for its cobbled streets and its association with the Brontë sisters – Charlotte, Emily and Anne, who came to live here in 1820. The Brontës were a close-knit family and their home, now the **Parsonage Museum,** formed the focus of the sisters' world from an early age. The museum displays the Brontës' own furniture and possessions, and is a good starting point for the popular Brontë Trail.
www.visithaworth.com

✚ 3G 🛈 2–4 West Lane ☎ 01535 642329

Brontë Parsonage Museum

✉ Church Street ☎ 01535 642323 🕔 Apr–Oct daily 10–5.30, Oct–Mar daily 11–5 💷 Moderate 🍴 Cafés in town (£–££)

HEBDEN BRIDGE

Although the town dates back to medieval times when it developed at the intersection of trade routes and a river crossing, it wasn't until mechanisation was introduced in the 18th century that Hebden Bridge began to grow. As its textile industry flourished, the influx of workers meant that houses had to be built up the steep valley sides, giving the town its characteristic 'double-decker' housing. Some of the old mill buildings have been attractively converted into museums, craft galleries and shopping areas. At the heart of the South Pennines, the surrounding landscape of Calderdale, overlooked by the tower on

Stoodley Pike, is surprisingly attractive.

✚ 3G 🛈 New Road ☎ 01422 843831
🕐 Easter–Oct daily Mon–Fri 9.30–5.30, Sat 10.15–5, Sun 10.30–5; Nov–Easter Mon–Fri 10–5, Sat–Sun 10.30–4.15

HOLY ISLAND

It was on Holy Island, formerly known as Lindisfarne, that St Aidan of Iona founded a monastery in the 7th century, **Lindisfarne Priory,** one of the holiest sites of Anglo-Saxon England. This small island is only accessible by causeway from Beal, and only then when tides permit. St Cuthbert lived and died on the island, which has become a place of pilgrimage. Lindisfarne Castle was built in the 16th century, to defend the harbour from marauding Scots, and its museum includes a collection of inscribed stones, all that remain of the first monastery.

✚ 3M

Lindisfarne Priory and Museum
☎ 01289 389200 🕐 Apr–Sep daily 9.30–5; Oct 9.30–4; Nov–Jan 10–2; Feb–Mar 9.30–4. Closed 24–26 Dec, 1 Jan ✋ Moderate 🍴 Café and restaurant in village (£)

KENDAL

The limestone-grey buildings of this busy market town conceal a maze of yards and 'ginnels' (narrow passages). They are a delight to explore: one contains a row of charming almshouses, still in use. Above the town rise the ruins of Kendal Castle, birthplace of Katherine Parr (1512–48), the last wife of Henry VIII. **Abbot Hall Art Gallery,** near the church, includes works by Ruskin, Constable and Turner. The Museum of Lakeland Life in the adjacent stables contains Arthur Ransome and 'Postman Pat' memorabilia, as well as local history displays.

www.lakelandgateway.info

➕ 2J 🛈 Town Hall, Highgate ☎ 01539 725758;
🕐 Mon–Sat 9–5, Sun 10–4

Abbott Hall Art Gallery

☎ 01539 722464; www.abbothall.org.uk
🕐 Apr–Oct daily 10.30–5; Nov–Mar daily 10.30–4.
Closed Sun, 25 Dec–early Feb ✋ Moderate
🍴 The Coffee Shop (£)

LAKE DISTRICT

See pages 44–45.

LANCASTER

Once an important port for the slave trade, much of Lancaster's character comes from the Georgian buildings of this unhappy period, though there was much traffic in mahogany, tobacco, rum and sugar, too. **Lancaster Castle,** built around 1200 and strengthened in the 15th century, dominates

the city and is still used as a crown court and prison, but some sections are open to the public, including the cells where the Pendle Witches were imprisoned. The shopping centre contains many historic buildings, including the Judges' Lodging, now a museum, featuring the finely crafted furniture of the local family, the Gillows.

✚ 2H 🚹 29 Castle Hill ☎ 01524 32878 🕗 Apr–Nov Mon–Sat 10–5; Nov–Apr Mon–Sat 10–4

Lancaster Castle

✉ The Shire Hall ☎ 01524 64998; www.lancastercastle.com
🕗 Mid-Mar to mid-Dec times vary 👜 Inexpensive 🍴 Folly Café, Castle Hill (£) ❓ Weekend tours every 30 mins from 10.30–4

LEEDS

The largest urban development in Yorkshire and its economic capital, Leeds owes its growth, notably during the 19th century, to wool and to its position as a port on the Leeds–Liverpool and Aire and Calder canals. The area around the canals, which run through the city centre, has been developed to provide a lively waterfront culture of pavement cafés and specialist shops along the water's edge. Following large-scale urban rejuvenation, Leeds has become an outstanding nightlife destination and a major cultural centre, home to Opera North. Leeds' shopping is also a major draw; try the fashionable department store Harvey Nichols for window shopping.

www.leeds.gov.uk

✚ 3G 🚹 The Arcade, City Railway Station ☎ 0113 242 5242 🕗 Tue–Sat 9–5.30, Mon 10–5.30, Sun 10–4

LEVENS HALL AND TOPIARY GARDENS

This magnificent Elizabethan mansion is built around a 13th-century tower, and is the family home of the Bagots. On display is a collection of Jacobean furniture, paintings and early English patchwork. The award-winning topiary gardens were laid out in 1694, and feature yews trimmed to the shape of pyramids, peacocks and hats.

www.levenshall.co.uk

✚ 2H ☎ 01539 560321 ⏱ House: 12–4.30. Gardens: 10–4.30 ✋ Moderate

🍴 Tea room (£–££)

LIVERPOOL

The city that produced the Beatles is also renowned for its acerbic wit, a remarkable community spirit and fiercely proud loyalty to one of its two major football teams. Liverpool rose to prominence through trade with the Americas, importing sugar, spices, tobacco and slaves. Its historic waterfront is now an important tourist attraction, centred on Albert Dock, where the warehouses comprise probably the greatest grouping of Grade I Listed buildings in the country.

They have been converted into a complex of shops, television studios, bars, restaurants and the Tate Gallery Liverpool, which houses an impressive collection of contemporary art. It is complemented by the **Walker Art Gallery,** with its collection of European Old Masters, pre-Raphaelite and modern British works.
www.visitliverpool.com

➕ 1F 🛈 Atlantic Pavilion, Albert Dock ☎ 0906 680 6886; 🕓 Daily 9–5.30

Walker Art Gallery

✉ William Brown Street ☎ 0151 478 4199; www.thewalker.org.uk 🕓 Daily 10–5. Closed 1 Jan, 23–26 Dec 🖐 Moderate 🍴 The Walker Coffee Shop (£)

MANCHESTER

Once the world's major cotton-milling centre, Manchester, with its spruced-up Victorian buildings, extensive shopping, plentiful restaurants and enviable nightlife, is arguably one of the trendiest places in England. Manchester has undergone an urban makeover unequalled in Britain, boosted by the phenomenal success of the Manchester United football team. The area known as Castlefield, site of a Roman fort, is today the focus of Manchester's tourism industry. Many of the surrounding Victorian warehouses have been converted into apartments, hotels and tourist attractions.
Urbis is a new kind of museum in a dramatic glass building with interactive exhibits about life in cities around the world.
www.visitmanchester.com

➕ 2F 🛈 Town Hall Extension, Lloyd Street ☎ 0871 222 8223 🕓 Mon–Sat 10–5.30, Sun 10.30–4.30

Urbis

✉ Cathedral Gardens ☎ 0161 605 8200; www.urbis.org.uk 🕓 Sun–Wed 10–6, Thu–Sat 10–8 🖐 Moderate 🍴 Conservatory Café (£–££)

NATIONAL COAL MINING MUSEUM

This award-winning museum offers guided tours underground allowing visitors to see the methods and conditions of mining from the early 1800s. There are extensive indoor and outdoor displays, a working steam winder, a train ride and pit ponies.

www.ncm.org.uk

✚ 3G ✉ Caphouse Colliery, New Road, Overton, Wakefield ☎ 01924 848806 🕐 Daily 10–5 ✋ Moderate

NEWCASTLE UPON TYNE

Capital of northeast England, Newcastle has survived the decline in many of its traditional industries, such as ship building and coal mining. The oldest part of the city is Quayside, now a fashionable oasis with restaurants, pubs and antique shops. The 'new castle' dates from the time of William I (the Conqueror, reigned 1066–87), though the city's economic wealth grew from a regional monopoly on coal exportation introduced in Elizabethan times. The city has several galleries and theatres, including the **Laing Gallery,** which focuses on 19th-century art.

www.visitnewcastlegateshead.com

✚ 3K ℹ 132 Grainger Street and Guildhall, Quayside 🕐 Mon–Fri 9.30–5.30, Sat 9–5.30 ☎ 0191 277 8000

Laing Gallery

✉ New Bridge Street ☎ 0191 232 7734 🕐 Mon–Sat 10–4.50, Sun 2–4.50; www.twmuseums.org.uk ✋ Free 🍴 The Café Laing (£–££)

NORTH OF ENGLAND OPEN AIR MUSEUM, BEAMISH

Buildings from all over the region have been reassembled at Beamish. The museum vividly illustrates life in the northeast of England in the early 1800s and 1900s, and includes a colliery village, a 19th-century manor, and a north country town.

www.beamish.org.uk

✚ 3K ✉ Beamish, Co Durham ☎ 0191 370 4000; 🕐 Apr–Oct daily 10–5; Nov–Mar Sat–Sun, Tue–Thu 10–4 ✋ Expensive 🍴 Tea room (£–££)

RICHMOND

This town is a gem, an open-air museum of the grandest kind, dominated by its outstanding castle, built by the first Earl of Richmond, Alan Rufus. Centred on a huge cobbled market square with radiating wynds (narrow alleys), Richmond contains numerous Georgian buildings, but its most unusual building is the defunct Holy Trinity Church, which houses the Green Howards regimental museum.

www.yorkshiredales.org

✚ 3J 🛈 Friary Gardens, Victoria Road ☎ 01748 850252; ⏰ Easter–Oct daily 9.30–5; Nov–Mar Mon–Sat 9.30–4.30

🍴 Numerous in town (£–£££)

SALTAIRE

Built between 1852 and 1872 by Sir Titus Salt, this village on the River Aire is a perfectly preserved vision of his industrial Utopia, modelled on buildings of the Italian Renaissance. It was originally constructed in open countryside, to provide Salt's mill workers with the benefits of fresh air, though it is now surrounded by urban sprawl. The mill, which is larger than St Paul's Cathedral in London, was once the biggest factory in the world, and was the centre of a small conglomeration of schools, hospitals, houses, parks, baths and washhouses. The **1853 Gallery** displays the world's largest collection of the works of Bradford-born artist, David Hockney.

✚ 3G 🛈 2 Victoria Road ☎ 01274 774993 ⏰ Daily 10–6

1853 Gallery

✉ Salts Mill, Victoria Road ☎ 01274 531163; www.saltsmill.org.uk

⏰ Mon–Fri 10–5.30, Sat–Sun 10–6. Closed 25–26 Dec 🎟 Free

SHEFFIELD

Until 1997, Sheffield was as far from a tourist destination as you could imagine. Then came the smash hit film *The Full Monty*, a tale of unemployed steelworkers-turned-male-strippers, set in Sheffield and suddenly the town was brought into the limelight.

The **Kelham Island Museum,** a mile or so north of the city centre, tells the story of Sheffield, its industry and life, and houses the largest working steam engine in Britain. Reconstructed workshops, working cutlers and craftspeople demonstrate the traditional 'Made in Sheffield' skills, and there's a 'hands-on' experience for children to discover how steel is made, as well as interactive exhibits about energy. Getting around Sheffield is easy if you use the new Supertram service, which rumbles around the city centre.

www. sheffieldcity.co.uk

✚ 3F 🚩 1 Tudor Square

🕐 Mon–Sun 8–6

☎ 0114 221 1900;

Kelham Island Museum

✉ Alma Street, Sheffield

☎ 0114 272 2106;

www.simt.co.uk

🕐 Mon–Thu 10–4, Sun 11–4.45. Closed Fri–Sat

✋ Moderate 🍴 Café (£)

SIZERGH CASTLE

The ancestral home of the Strickland family for over 760 years, Sizergh Castle, near Kendal, is built around a 14th-century tower, which was extended in Elizabethan times. The castle is surrounded by attractive gardens and contains some fine examples of oak furniture and carved wooden chimney-pieces.

✚ 2H ☎ 015395 60070 ⧀ Castle: Easter–Oct Sun–Thu 1–4.30. Gardens 12.30–5.30 ✋ Moderate 🍴 Tea room (£)

SKIPTON

At the southern edge of the Yorkshire Dales National Park (➤ 54–55), the market town of Skipton is commonly known as the 'gateway to the Dales', and traces its history back to the 7th century when it was known as Sceptone, or 'Sheeptown'. It is dominated by **Skipton Castle** at the top of the main street, which was reconstructed in the 14th century and remodelled by the formidable Lady Anne Clifford in the 17th century. Canal trips are

available on the Leeds–Liverpool Canal which passes through the Skipton which is a fine base for exploring the southern Dales.
www.skiptononline.co.uk

✚ 3G 🛈 35 Coach Street ☎ 01756 792809 🕓 Mon–Sat 10–5 (10–4 in winter), Sun 11–3 (closed in winter)

Skipton Castle

☎ 01756 792442; www.skiptoncastle.co.uk
🕓 Mar–Oct Mon–Sat 10–6, Sun 12–6; Oct–Feb Mon–Sat 10–4, Sun 12–4 ✋ Moderate 🍴 Tea room (£)

WHITBY

Associations with Captain Cook, the atmospheric ruins of a 13th-century abbey, a fishing harbour and quiet charm all combine to make Whitby an agreeable and fascinating place to visit. All Cook's ships were built here, and the home of John Walker, to whom Cook was apprenticed, has been converted into the **Captain Cook Memorial Museum.** The abbey stands by St Mary's Church on the clifftop above the east side of the town. The church is reached by the 199 steps of the Church Stairs, which featured in Bram Stoker's Dracula. A Dracula Trail can be followed across the town.
www.discoveryorkshirecoast.com

✚ 5J 🛈 Langbourne Road ☎ 01723 383636 🕓 May–Sep daily 9.30–6; Oct–Apr 9.30–4.30

Captain Cook Memorial Museum

✉ Grape Lane ☎ 01947 601900 🕓 Mar–Nov daily 9.45–5 ✋ Moderate

YORK

See pages 52–53.

YORKSHIRE DALES

See pages 54–55.

HOTELS

Haleys Hotel and Restaurant (££)

An elegant Victorian town house hotel just over a mile from Leeds city centre. It boasts one of the best restaurants in Leeds.

✉ Shire Oak Road, Headingley, Leeds ☎ 0113 278 4446

Le Meridien Victoria and Albert (££–£££)

See page 73.

Le Meridien York (££–£££)

See page 73.

Miller Howe (££)

An established part of the Lakeland scene with an international reputation. Many bedrooms have private balconies overlooking Lake Windermere. Dinner is a unique experience.

✉ Rayrigg Road, Windermere, Cumbria ☎ 015394 42536

The Royal (££)

A listed Georgian building situated at Waterloo. The hotel looks out over Liverpool Bay and has modern, well-equipped bedrooms.

✉ Marine Terrace, Waterloo, Liverpool ☎ 0151 928 2332

Shap Wells Hotel (££)

Cumbria's largest family-owned hotel, set in secluded, wooded ground midway between Kendal and Penrith, and only five minutes from junction 39 on the M6. An ideal from which to explore the Lake District and Yorkshire Dales.

✉ Shap, Penrith, Cumbria ☎ 01931 716628

Simonstone Hall Country House Hotel (££)

With lovely views over the Wensleydale countryside, this hotel is conveniently situated for exploring the Yorkshire Dales. Has a warm, friendly atmosphere and prettily decorated rooms.

✉ Simonstone, Hawes, North Yorkshire ☎ 01969 667255

Vermont Hotel (££–£££)

Friendly and stylish hotel next to the castle and conveniently located in the very heart of the buzzing quayside area.

✉ Castle Garth, Newcastle upon Tyne ☎ 0191 233 1010

RESTAURANTS

Anthony's (££–£££)

See page 58.

Gianfranco (£–££)

A long-established Italian restaurant with some attractive lunchtime and 'happy hour' menus.

✉ 6–10 Leazes Park Road, Newcastle upon Tyne ☎ 0191 222 0659

🕔 Daily lunch, dinner

The Glass House (£–££)

See page 58.

The Inn at Whitewell (££)

Tremendously popular and beautifully situated in the Forest of Bowland, the inn is surrounded by rolling wooded hills.

✉ Whitewell, Forest of Bowland, Lancashire ☎ 01200 448222

🕔 Daily 12–2, 7.30–9

Sharrow Bay (£££)

Among the top places to eat in the Lake District. Stay in the hotel if you can and let the atmosphere take over.

✉ Sharrow Bay, Howtown, Cumbria ☎ 017684 86301 🕔 Daily lunch (from 12.30), dinner (from 7.30); closed Dec–late Feb

Simply Heathcote's (£££)

Stylish and sophisticated, minimalist eatery serving modern British cuisine.

✉ Beetham Plaza, 25 The Strand, Liverpool ☎ 0151 236 3536 🕔 Mon–Fri 12–2.30, 6–10; Sat 12–2.30, 6–11; Sun 12–9

St William's College Restaurant (££)

Candlelight and jazz, and a historic building next to the Minster, make this one of York's most popular eating places.

✉ 5 College Street, York ☎ 01904 634830 🕐 Mon–Sat 10–5, 6–9, Sun lunch only

Village Bakery (£)

Award-winning organic bakery and café in a converted barn, at the foot of the Pennines. Breakfasts are large and splendid.

✉ Melmerby, near Penrith, Cumbria ☎ 01768 881515 🕐 Mon–Sat 8.30–5, Sun 9.30–5. Check for winter opening times

ENTERTAINMENT

Bridgewater Hall

Recitals by the Hallé Orchestra and the BBC Philharmonic, plus one-off shows.

✉ Lower Mosley Street, Manchester ☎ 0161 907 9000

Everyman Theatre

From Shakespeare to stand-up comedy.

✉ 1 Hope Street, Liverpool ☎ 0151 709 4776

Grand Theatre and Opera House

Opera North and full range of theatrical productions.

✉ Briggate, Leeds ☎ 0113 222 6222

Northern Stage

Modern theatre and performances by the Northern Stage Company.

✉ Barras Bridge, Newcastle ☎ 0191 230 5151

Philharmonic Hall

Concerts by the renowned Royal Liverpool Philharmonic orchestra.

✉ Hope Street, Liverpool ☎ 0151 709 3789

Royal Northern College of Music

Quality modern jazz concerts.

✉ 124 Oxford Road, Manchester ☎ 0161 907 5200

Central England

The 'Heart of England' is easy to reach and explore. Throughout the region, which extends from Derbyshire in the north to Worcestershire and Warwickshire in the south, you'll find a wealth of historic houses, castles and stately homes, whose design and antique treasures are rivalled only by the splendour of the grounds within which they are set.

You'll find outstanding opportunities to take part in, or watch, sport, to enjoy a wide-ranging cuisine and to explore the bustling regional cities such as Derby, Nottingham, Leicester, Birmingham and Coventry. Central England is relatively unfrequented by visitors, so it's perhaps here that you have the greatest opportunity of finding a taste of real England...probably tea-flavoured!

BIRMINGHAM

Birmingham's reputation is grim, but once you escape New Street station, Digbeth bus station or the chaotic ring roads, you'll find a city full of vitality, especially in the award-winning waterfront development in Brindley Place, built around the old canal network. The 'city of 1001 trades' was the proving ground for the founders of the Industrial Revolution – steam pioneers James Watt and Matthew Bolton, the inventor of gas lighting William Murdock, and chemist John Priestley. Now again facing a huge city centre transformation, Birmingham's story can be found in the city's excellent museums and galleries, among which the state-of-the-art **National Sea Life Centre** and the **Birmingham Museum and Art Gallery** in Chamberlain Square are worth singling out.

England's second city, Birmingham today is a major jewellery manufacturing centre, and the Jewellery Quarter is a good place to explore. You can walk there from the city centre in about a quarter of an hour, or take a train from Moor Street.

www.beinbirmingham.com

➕ 2D 🛈 130 Colmore Row, Victoria Square ☎ 0121 202 5099 🕓 Daily 9.15–5.30

National Sea Life Centre

✉ Brindley Place ☎ 0121 643 6777 🕓 Mon–Fri 10–4, Sat–Sun 10–5 💷 Expensive

Birmingham Museum and Art Gallery

✉ Chamberlain Square ☎ 0121 303 2834; www.bmag.org.uk 🕓 Mon–Thu, Sat 10–5, Fri 10.30–5, Sun 12.30–5 💷 Free

BLENHEIM PALACE

The imposing 18th-century palace of Blenheim is the family seat of the Duke of Marlborough and was designed by Sir John Vanbrugh. It contains several rooms dedicated to Sir Winston Churchill, the wartime prime minister, who was born here and is buried in the church at Bladon, not far away. The nearby village of Woodstock has royal associations dating from Saxon times when the area was used as a hunting ground.

www.blenheimpalace.com

 13R ✉ Woodstock, Oxfordshire ☎ 0870 060 2080 ◷ Feb–Oct daily 9 or 10.30–5; Nov–Dec Wed–Sun 9 or 10.30–5 ✋ Expensive

BRIDGNORTH

Bridgnorth, on the River Severn, was once an important port. The old walled town (High Town) is built on a sandstone cliff and linked to the Low Town by the oldest and steepest

inland funicular in England. Check out the old Town Hall, which has some stunning stained glass.

   The station is now the northern terminus of the Severn Valley Railway, Britain's longest restored standard-gauge line which runs steam trains to Kidderminster.

www.bridgenorthshropshire.com

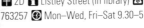 2D ℹ Listley Street (in library) ☎ 01746 763257 ◷ Mon–Wed, Fri–Sat 9.30–5

BUXTON

There's a relaxing and genteel air about Buxton (named *Aquae Arnemetiae* by the Romans), one of the highest market towns in England. It even has its own natural spring, the source of its 18th-century popularity, which you can see in the Natural Mineral Baths. You can help yourself to mineral water from St Anne's Well, next to the Pump Room, which houses an art gallery. Although the 5th Duke of Devonshire's grand design to make Buxton rival Bath and Cheltenham as a spa resort never quite made it, the plan did see the construction of some distinguished buildings, of which The Crescent, modelled on Bath's Royal Crescent, is a fine example. **Poole's Cavern,** to the southwest, is worth exploring for its

stalactites and stalagmites, and a short walk from there to a 19th-century folly, Solomon's Temple, provides a fine view over the town. **www.**visitbuxton.co.uk

➕ 3F 🛈 The Crescent ☎ 01298 25106 🕓 Mar–Oct daily 9.30–5; Nov–Feb 10–4
Poole's Cavern

✉ Buxton Country Park ☎ 01298 26978; www.poolescavern.co.uk 🕓 Mar–Oct daily 10–5 👋 Moderate 🍴 Shop selling coffees and teas

CASTLETON

Dominated by the imposing ruins of Peveril Castle, the neat village of Castleton is popular both with walkers, who come to enjoy this part of the Peak District and visitors who come to explore the subterranean world of its caverns – The Peak, Treak Cliff, Speedwell and Blue John. **Peveril Castle,** from which the town gets its name, sits high above Cave Dale and gazes across the valley to an Iron-Age fort on the imposing, but crumbling, Mam Tor.

🚻 3F 🛈 Castle Street ☎ 01433 620679 🕐 Mar–Nov daily 9.30–5.30;
Dec–Feb daily 10–5

Peveril Castle

✉ Market Place ☎ 01433 620613 ✋ Inexpensive 🕐 Apr daily 10–5;
May–Aug daily 10–6; Sep–Nov daily 10–5; Dec–Mar Thu–Mon 10–4

CHATSWORTH HOUSE

The home of the Dukes of Devonshire for over 400 years,
Chatsworth is among the finest houses in England, and contains
one of the richest collections of fine and decorative art in private
hands, including works by Tintoretto and Rembrandt. The massive
formal gardens are tiny in comparison to the enormous park,
designed by Capability Brown, which surrounds the house.

www.chatsworthhouse.org

🚻 3F ✉ Bakewell ☎ 01246 582204 🕐 Late Mar to mid-Dec, daily 11–5.30
✋ Expensive 🍴 Carriage House Restaurant (£–££) and cafés

CHESTER

Encircled by medieval and Roman walls (around which there is an informative tour), the heart of Chester is the cluster of Tudor and Victorian buildings that includes the raised arcades of The Rows. This is very much a county town, and an ideal base from which to explore. The Romans built their largest fortress in Britain here, but it was much later, as trade routes with Ireland opened up, that the prosperity of the town grew. The cathedral, built between 1250 and 1540, suffers from Victorian meddling, but remains a commanding feature, worth visiting. Beyond the city walls you can cruise on the River Dee, or rent rowing boats, while further afield, **Chester Zoo,** on the A41, 3 miles (5km) north of the city, is England's largest.

➕ 1F 🛈 Town Hall, Northgate Street and Vicars Lane ☎ 01244 402111 🕐 Apr–Oct Mon–Fri 9.30–5.30, Sat 9.30–5.30, Sun 10–4; Oct–Marr Mon 9.30–5, Sun 10.30–3.30

Chester Zoo

☎ 01244 380280; www.chesterzoo.org 🕐 Daily from 10, but closing variable throughout year ✋ Expensive 🍴 Oasis Café and Oakfield Restaurant (£–££)

HADDON HALL

Haddon Hall is a Tudor manor house with Norman and Saxon origins, and has served as the setting for several films. During the 18th and 19th centuries the hall was virtually abandoned and fell into neglect, which proved to be a saving grace, for it evaded the attentions of the Georgian and Victorian 'improvers'. Most of what you see today dates from the 14th and 15th centuries.

www.haddonhall.co.uk

➕ 3F 🖂 Bakewell, Derbyshire ☎ 01629 812855
🕓 Apr and Oct Sat–Mon 12–5; May–Sep daily 12–5
✋ Expensive 🍴 Restaurant (£–££)

HEREFORD

Hereford lies amid beautiful countryside and has been a cathedral city since the 8th century. Indeed it is the Norman **cathedral** which is the town's real draw. It has the world's largest chained library (with books and manuscripts from the 8th to the 15th centuries), and the Mappa Mundi, a parchment map from 1289, depicting the world radiating from Jerusalem.

➕ 1C

Cathedral

☎ 01432 374200 🕓 Mappa Mundi exhibition: Mon–Sat 10–4.30, Sun 11–4
✋ Cathedral free; exhibition moderate 🍴 Cloisters Café

IRONBRIDGE GORGE

Ironbridge Gorge, the crucible of the Industrial Revolution, is Britain's best centre for industrial archaeology, and today enjoys World Heritage Site status. Centred around the eponymous iron bridge, ten **museums,** which it can take a couple of days to explore, illuminate Abraham Darby's pioneering iron work and life in an industrial region. Best among these are the Museum of the

Gorge, the Coalbrookdale Museum of Iron, where it all started, the Coalport China Museum, and the Jackfield Tile Museum, which houses a unique display of Victorian tiles. A 'passport ticket' is available which allows you to visit all the sites economically.

www.ironbridge.org.uk

➕ 2D ⓘ Ironbridge ☎ 01952 433522/884391 ⓒ Daily 10–5

Ironbridge Gorge Museums

☎ 01952 433522 ⓒ Daily 10–5. Some museums closed Nov–Mar, all closed 1 Jan, 24–25 Dec ✋ Moderate–expensive

KENILWORTH CASTLE

Immortalized by writer Sir Walter Scott, Kenilworth, and the castle from which he took his inspiration, is predominantly a dormitory of Coventry, but the castle is remarkable. Begun in the 12th century, it eventually fell into the hands of John of Gaunt, who turned it into a magnificent fortified home. His son, Henry IV, used it as a royal residence, and so it remained until Elizabeth I gave it to her much favoured court advisor Robert Dudley, Duke of Northumberland. These red sandstone ruins are still extensive and imposing.

➕ 3D ☎ 01926 852078 ⓒ Apr–Sep daily 10–6; Oct daily 10–5; Nov–Mar daily 10–4 ✋ Moderate 🍴 Tea room, Leicester's Barn (£)

LICHFIELD

The medieval market town of Lichfield, birthplace of the 17th-century writer Dr Samuel Johnson, is dominated by its distinctive three-spired cathedral which dates back over 1,000 years. The town centre has a grid of medieval streets overlaid with later, mostly 18th-century, development and makes for fascinating exploration. Worth seeking out are the Samuel Johnson Museum on Market Square, and the museum commemorating Erasmus Darwin (grandfather of Charles) on Beacon Street.

www.visitlichfield.com

➕ 3D ⓘ Lichfield Garrick Arts and Business Venue ☎ 01543 412121 ⓒ Mon–Sat 9–6

LINCOLN

The magnificent triple-towered cathedral of Lincoln dominates the landscape from every approach; it is the third largest church in Britain. The site, on a rocky hill rising from the River Witham on the northwest edge of the Fens, was first occupied by Celts, and was such an important, strategic position that the Romans built one of their four regional capitals of Britain here. Lincoln Castle was built over the original Roman town and uses some of the Roman walls. The Jew's House on Steep Hill, now a top restaurant, is one of the best examples of 12th-century domestic architecture.

www.lincoln.goc.uk

⊞ 4E 🛈 9 Castle Hill ☎ 01522 873213
🕐 Mon–Thu 9.30–5.30, Fri 9.30–5,
Sat–Sun 10–5

LUDLOW

One of England's best-preserved medieval and Georgian towns, Ludlow is a place of endless fascination. The town's Norman castle stands in a commanding position on a hill almost surrounded by rivers. The church, St Laurence's, contains some magnificent misericords, and is a testament to the former wool-trading prosperity of

the town. Timber-framed houses and fine Georgian buildings line all the streets, and make this a delightful place to wander. Castle lovers take the short journey northwards to visit **Stokesay,** the best-preserved 13th-century fortified manor house in England.

www.ludlow.org.uk

🔹 1D 🏛 Castle Street ☎ 01584 875053 🕐 Mon–Sat 10–5; summer Sun 10.30–5

Stokesay Castle

✉ South of Craven Arms off 🔹 49 ☎ 01588 672544; www.english-heritage 🕐 Variable, see website for full details ✋ Moderate

LYME PARK

Set in a vast woodland deer park with ornamental gardens, Lyme Hall was transformed from a Tudor house into an excellent Italianate palace by the Venetian architect, Leoni. The park and hall were also used as the setting for Pemberley in the BBC's adaptation of Austen's *Pride and Prejudice*.

🔹 2F ✉ Disley, Stockport ☎ 01663 762023, 01663 766492 (recording) 🕐 Apr–Oct Fri–Tue 1–5 (hall), 8–8.30 (park); Nov–Mar 8–6 (park only) ✋ Moderate 🍴 Tea room (£)

MALVERN

Malvern is the generic name for a delightful string of towns along the base of the Malvern Hills, themselves famed for their water. The main centre is Great Malvern, dominated by its priory which has some splendid stained glass. The nearby Malvern Hills were inspiration for the great composer Edward Elgar (1857–1934) who was born not far away, near Worcester, and is buried at Little Malvern.

www.malvernhills.gov.uk

🚌 2C 🛈 21 Church Street ☎ 01684 892289 🕐 Daily 10–5 (Sun in winter 10–4)

MUCH WENLOCK

The Tudor, Jacobean and Georgian architecture in this quiet little town is perfectly reflected in the Guildhall, perched solidly on the ancient oak columns of the Butter Market. On the edge of town are the ruins of **Wenlock Priory,** an early 13th-century church.

🚌 1D

Wenlock Priory

☎ 01952 727466 🕐 May–Jun daily 10–5; Jul–Aug daily 10–6; Sep–Oct Thu–Mon 10–5; Nov–Feb Thu–Sun 10–4; Mar–Apr Thu–Mon 10–5 🎫 Inexpensive

NOTTINGHAM

Built on sandstone hills at a crossing point of the River Trent, Nottingham is renowned for its association with the 13th-century freebooter, Robin Hood (Sherwood Forest; ➤ 130). This is one of England's biggest cities, and is a lively, buzzing place, with a good, if changeable, nightlife, and excellent shopping facilities. The site of the castle, demolished after the Civil War, and the old lace market are the most interesting places, along with the man-made caves, dating from medieval times, which are most easily accessible through the Broad Marsh shopping centre. Allow spare time for the Brewhouse Yard Museum on Castle Boulevard, which re-creates 19th-century life . There are many claimants to be the oldest pub in Britain, but Ye Olde Trip to Jerusalem (➤ 140), hacked from the walls below the castle, has a stronger claim than most, and was in use at the time of the 13th-century Crusades. DH Lawrence fans will find his birthplace museum in Eastwood, worth the 10-mile (16km) trip to see it.

www.visitnotts.com

🔲 4E 🛈 1–4 Smithy Row ☎ 0115 915 5330; ⏰ Sep–Jun Mon–Fri 9–5.30, Sat 9–5; Jul–Aug Mon–Fri 9–5.30, Sat 9–5, Sun 10–4

OXFORD

See pages 46–47.

QUARRY BANK MILL, STYAL

A working Georgian cotton mill, built in 1784 by Samuel Greg, which provides a wonderful insight into the early years of the Industrial Revolution. The group of buildings developed around a 50-ton waterwheel, and charts the growth of cotton textile manufacture. The mill is within the Styal Country Park.

www.quarrybankmill.org.uk

🏠 2F ✉ Styal, Wilmslow ☎ 01625 527468 🕐 Estate: daily 7–6. Apprentice House: mid-Mar to–Sep Tue–Sun; Oct to early Mar Wed–Sun; times vary
✋ Moderate 🍽 Mill Kitchen restaurant Mill Pantry (£)

SHERWOOD FOREST

Little remains of Robin Hood's Sherwood Forest except the 450 acres (182ha) of the present country park. Extensive clearance during the 18th century makes it hard to imagine how this meagre swathe of woodland ever concealed a band of outlaws.

Just a few minutes from the visitor centre is the Major Oak, more than 30ft (10m) in diameter, where Maid Marion and Robin pledged their undying love. There may be a lot of legend, folklore, tradition and just plain fibbing about the tales of this hero, but no one ever let that stop them having a good time.

Just north of Sherwood Forest is an area known as the Dukeries, and here you will find **Clumber Park,** a wide expanse of parkland and woods. Clumber was once the home of the Dukes of Newcastle, and though the house was demolished in 1938, many features of the estate remain, including a Gothic Revival chapel.

🏠 4E

Sherwood Forest Country Park Visitor Centre

✉ Edwinstowe ☎ 01623 823202 🕐 Mar–Oct daily 10–5; Nov–Feb daily 10–4

Clumber Park

☎ 01909 476592 🕐 Park: daily during daylight hours. Garden: Apr–Oct Mon–Fri 10–5, Sat–Sun 10–6 ✋ Pedestrians free; cars moderate
🍽 Restaurant (£–££)

SHREWSBURY

The River Severn determined Shrewsbury's siting, its development and its present character. The Saxon town of Scrobbesbyrig was built within a natural moat provided by a tight loop of the river, completely encircled except for a small gap – 'islanded in Severn stream', as A E Housman put it. Shrewsbury is the county town of Shropshire and claims to be the finest Tudor town in England. It's a crazy mish-mash of

medieval streets, half-timbered buildings and modern shops. Among the town's most interesting buildings are the red sandstone abbey (just on the edge of town) and the Market Hall, opposite the information centre, built in 1596 for the sale of woollen cloth. But you'll find more intriguing places along Grope Lane, Butcher Row and around St Alkmund's Church. One of the town's more famous sons is Charles Darwin. He attended Shrewsbury School, a splendid building founded by Edward VI in 1552.

www.visitshrewsbury.com

🏠 1E 🛈 The Square ☎ 01743 281200 ⏰ May–Sep Mon–Sat 9.30–5.30, Sun 10–4; Oct–Apr Mon–Sat 10–5; Easter Sun 10–4

STOKE-ON-TRENT

It is porcelain that justifies a visit to Stoke, an otherwise unattractive urban sprawl. Many of the world's most famous potteries developed here, thanks to the abundant presence of marl clay, coal, water, iron, copper and lead – the raw materials for the production of ceramics. Royal Doulton, Minton, Spode and Wedgwood all come from here. The city itself is an amalgam of six smaller towns – Stoke, Hanley, Tunstall, Longton, Burslem and Fenton. At the Gladstone Pottery Museum in Longton, local craftspeople demonstrate the skills of producing pottery and there are informative exhibits at the Royal Doulton Visitor Centre in Nile Street, Burslem; the World of Spode near the train station in Church Street, Stoke; the Wedgwood Visitor Centre in Barlaston; and the Potteries Museum in Bethesda Street, Hanley.

www.visitstoke.co.uk

🚻 2E 🛈 Victoria Hall, Bagnall Street ☎ 01782 236000 🕙 Mon–Sat 9.30–5.15

STRATFORD-UPON-AVON

The birthplace of William Shakespeare, Stratford-upon-Avon is one of the busiest tourist attractions outside London. Aside from the extensive theatre complexes (► 140), you can visit the Bard's birthplace, a half-timbered Tudor house, now restored as a museum, and his wife Anne Hathaway's pretty cottage in the nearby village of Shottery. The town itself is dominated by Shakespeare's legacy, and guided tours, on foot and by bus, are available.

Ask at the tourist information centre for details.

www.shakespeare-country.co.uk

🚻 3C 🛈 Bridgefoot, near bus station ☎ 0870 160 7930
🕙 Mon–Sat 9–5.30, Sun 10–4 ❓ Royal Shakespeare Company ☎ Box Office 0870 609 1110; www.rsc.org.uk

TATTON PARK

Tatton is one of the most complete historic estates to which the public has access. The Georgian Tatton Hall sits amid a landscaped deer park with woodland walks and bicycle trails, and is most opulently decorated, providing a fine setting for the Egerton family's collections of pictures, books, china, glass, silver and furniture. Victorian grandeur extends into the gardens where you'll find Japanese and Italian themes, a rose garden and a maze.

www.tattonpark.org.uk

✚ 2F ✉ Knutsford ☎ 01625 534400;
🕐 House: mid-Mar to Sep Tue–Sun 1–4.
Gardens: mid-Mar to Sep Tue–Sun 10–5. Park:
mid-Mar to Sep Mon–Sun 10–6; Oct–Apr
Tue–Sun 11–4 ✋ Moderate 🍴 Restaurant (££)

WARWICK CASTLE

Hailed as the finest medieval castle in England, the sheer size of Warwick Castle has you well on the way to believing it. And though there is much in the claim, a sizeable chunk of the castle dates from its 19th-century restoration, which turned the castle into a magnificent stately home. Nevertheless, it remains, a powerful and important piece of English architecture. The first building was Saxon, built in AD914 by Ethelfleda, daughter of Alfred the Great. This was followed by a wooden Norman castle, then the 14th-century stone version which remains today.

www.warwick-castle.co.uk

✚ 3C ☎ 0870 4422000 🕐 Apr–Sep daily 10–6; Oct–Mar daily 10–5
✋ Expensive 🍴 Café and restaurant

WORCESTER

Worcester, on the River Severn, first attained prominence during Roman times, when a flourishing iron smelting industry and a port were established here. Today, the city's glory is its cathedral, which has a history dating back to AD680, when a wooden cathedral is known to have existed here. There are other interesting buildings around the cathedral; don't miss the 14th-century Edgar Tower, the Kings' School buildings in College Green, the Deanery, the Watergate, the Old Palace or the ruins of Guesten Hall. The Commandery building dates from the 15th century. It served as Charles II's headquarters for a time and now functions as an excellent museum devoted to the Civil War. For many, Worcester's fame rests on the manufacture here of Royal Worcester porcelain (and also Worcestershire Sauce). The porcelain factory is not far from the river.

www.visitworcester.com

✚ 2C ℹ The Guildhall, High Street ☎ 01905 726311

a walk around Lathkill Dale

This is a linear walk visiting one of the most delightful of the Derbyshire dales. Check the times of the buses back to Bakewell from Youlgreave before you set out.

Walk up King Street and turn into South Church Street and then left onto Yeld Road. After 100yds (91m), turn right onto a flight of stone steps and, at the top, go up a driveway and then an alleyway. At the far end, go past houses and alongside a playing field. Cross a road and go along the right-hand edge of the school grounds, then, after two fields, turn left alongside a wall to reach a valley bottom. Turn right, and soon bear left onto a lane for Over Haddon. Go through Over Haddon, turning left at the end down to meet the River Lathkill. Turn right and walk up the valley for 2 miles (3.2km).

The first part of the dale is wooded, giving way to open, rocky scenery that typifies the contrasts of these dales.

As the dale narrows, cross a footbridge on the left and enter Cales Dale. After about 300yds (273m), cross the dale to climb steps on the other side, entering a sloping field. A well-marked route leads up to Calling Low Farm and across fields to a road. Turn left and immediately branch right, then right again behind a car park. Follow a lane down fields to a road below, and there turn left to follow the road into Youlgreave.

Take a little time to explore this lovely village before returning to Bakewell by bus (No. 171, ☎ 0870 608 2608). The bus stop is on the main street in Youlgreave.

Distance 6 miles (10km)
Time 3–4 hours including stops
Start point Bakewell 🚶 3F
End point Youlgreave
Lunch The Farmyard pub, Youlgreave (£–££)

HOTELS

Edgbaston Palace Hotel (££)

Built in 1854, the Edgbaston Palace Hotel is a Grade II listed building situated 1 mile (1.6km) from Birmingham city centre.

✉ 198 Hagley Road, Edgbaston, Birmingham ☎ 0121 452 1577

The Feathers at Ludlow (££)

See page 72.

Fownes Hotel (££)

The Victorian glove factory has been converted into a successful, modern hotel with restaurant and well-furnished bedrooms.

✉ City Walls Road, Worcester ☎ 01905 613151

Le Manoir aux Quat'Saisons (£££)

See page 73.

Quorn Country Hotel (££)

A pleasant hotel with lovely landscaped grounds sweeping down to the River Soar. There are choice of two restaurants.

✉ Charnwood House, Quorn, Leicestershire ☎ 01509 415050

Rutland Square Hotel (££)

An impressive conversion of a large red-brick warehouse, only 50yds (46m) from Nottingham Castle. The restaurant serves traditional English and French cuisine.

✉ St James Street, Nottingham ☎ 0115 941 1114

Tewkesbury Park Hotel and Country Club (££)

Set in 175 acres (71ha) of parkland, this hotel was built around an 18th-century mansion, and enjoys fine views of the River Severn.

✉ Lincoln Green Lane, Tewkesbury, Gloucestershire ☎ 0870 609 6101

Welcombe Hotel and Golf Course (£££)

Magnificent Jacobean-style mansion set in its own parkland with extensive formal gardens and 18-hole golf course.

✉ Warwick Road, Stratford-upon-Avon ☎ 01789 295252

RESTAURANTS

Chez Jules (££)
This decent French restaurant in the busy centre of Birmingham has an excellent line of lunchtime specials.
✉ 5a Ethel Street, Birmingham ☎ 0121 633 4664 🕐 Daily lunch, dinner; closed Sun dinner

Brown's (££)
See page 58.

The Eagle and Child (£)
Access to this pub is through the reception of the Royalist Hotel, the oldest inn in England. It serves traditional food and real ales.
✉ Stow on the Wold, Gloucestershire ☎ 01451 830670 🕐 Daily 12–2.30, 6–9.30

The George (£)
Overlooking the village green fringed by trees, and on the edge of picturesque Dovedale, the George is the focal point of the village. Low-beamed ceilings make for a cosy bar area while outside seating is ideal for summer dining.
✉ Alstonefield, Derbyshire ☎ 01335 310205 🕐 Daily 12–2, 7–9

Green's Café (£)
See page 58.

King Charles II (££)
Although the 17th-century ambience is slightly contrived, the King Charles II nevertheless serves outstanding traditional food.
✉ New Street, Worcester ☎ 01905 22449 🕐 Mon–Sat lunch, dinner

The Oppo (££)
The best value in a food-laden street, serving imaginative international cuisine in a buzzing atmosphere. Always busy, but an ideal place to eat if you're exploring Shrewsbury.
✉ 13 Sheep Street, Stratford-upon-Avon, Warwickshire ☎ 01789 269980 🕐 Daily lunch, dinner

Rose and Crown (£–££)
A fine town centre inn, good for an all-day range of inexpensive bar meals and snacks.

✉ Market Place, Warwick ☎ 01926 411 117 🕓 All day

Ye Olde Trip to Jerusalem (£–££)
Built into a rockface, this pub dates back to the 12th century.

✉ 1 Brewhouse Yard, Castle Road, Nottingham ☎ 0115 9473171
🕓 Daily 11–11

ENTERTAINMENT

Hippodrome Theatre
The home of Birmingham Royal Ballet and regularly hosting the Welsh National Opera.

✉ Hurst Street, Birmingham ☎ 0870 7305555

Midland Arts Centre
Well supported by touring theatre companies.

✉ Cannon Hill Park, Edgbaston, Birmingham ☎ 0121 440 3838

Playhouse
With the Holywell Music Room, provides the bulk of music and theatre in Oxford.

✉ Beaumont Street, Oxford ☎ 01865 305305; www.oxfordplayhouse.com

Stratford-upon-Avon Theatres
For all things Shakespearean, the Royal Shakespeare Theatre; for contemporary works as well as Shakespeare, The Swan; and for experimental works, The Other Place in Southern Lane.

☎ Box office: 0870 6091110; www.rsc.org.uk

Symphony Hall
The acclaimed City of Birmingham Symphony Orchestra, performs at the acoustically magnificent Symphony Hall, which is also the venue for a host of touring productions.

✉ International Convention Centre, Centenary Square, Birmingham
☎ 0121 780 3333

Southeast England

All along the south and east coasts of England, names and places ring significantly through the ages; the White Cliffs of Dover and the Seven Sisters, cliff faces defiant against the sea and continental Europe, are found here, as are villages rich in the traditions of the sea. Here you can explore quiet cobbled streets or elegant waterfronts or enjoy winding cliff-top paths.

The southeast of England has always been the invader's route into the country and the landscape bears testimony to this in its scars

and monuments. This '1066 country' embraces castles, battlefields and historic places, such as Leeds Castle in Kent, home to Henry VIII, or the ancient city of Canterbury, destination of Chaucer's pilgrims. The richness of the countryside unfolds before you into beautiful landscapes, earning Kent the epithet 'the Garden of England'.

BLICKLING HALL

Built in the 17th century, red-brick Blicking Hall is one of England's great Jacobean houses, famed for its spectacular long gallery, superb library and outstanding collection of furniture, pictures and tapestries. The gardens are splendid whatever the time of year, and the extensive surrounding parkland features a lake and many beautiful and relaxing walks. Concerts are held here in the summer and artists have included Westlife and Van Morrison.
www.nationaltrust.org.uk

🚩 18T 📧 Blickling, Norfolk ☎ 01263 738030 ⏰ House: Apr–Sep Wed–Sun 1–5; Oct Wed–Sun 1–4. Park: daily dawn–dusk 🖐 Moderate 🍴 Restaurant and pantry (£–££)

BODIAM CASTLE

Built in 1385, both as a defence and a home,
Bodiam Castle is one of the most famous
and evocative castles in Britain. The exterior
is virtually complete and the ramparts rise
dramatically above the moat. Enough of
the interior survives to give an impression
of castle life, and there are spiral staircases
and battlements to explore. A small
museum adds a social dimension.

www.nationaltrust.org.uk

🕂 16P ✉ Robertsbridge, East Sussex ☎ 01580
830436 ⏰ Feb–Oct daily 10.30–6; Nov–Jan Sat–Sun 10.30–4 (times may
vary) ✋ Moderate 🍴 Tea room (£)

BRIGHTON

In the late 18th century the Prince of Wales, later George IV,
visited Brighton and began the trend for seaside holidays. The
seafront boasts elegant cream-coloured Regency terraces that
extend to neighbouring Hove, but the city's most famous building
is the extraordinary Indian-style Pavilion. Today, Brighton has
become a bohemian city with a large student population and gay
community and is known for its nightlife. For a glimpse of its roots
and good shopping, head to The Lanes, a maze of narrow
alleyways with interesting boutiques, antique shops, cafés and

restaurants. North Laine
has pubs, cafés and
quirky shops selling
1950s kitsch.

www.visitbrighton.com

🕂 15P 🏠 10 Bartholomew
Square ☎ 0906 7112255
⏰ Mon–Sat 10–5; summer
Mon–Sat 10–5, Sun 10–4

BURY ST EDMUNDS

Bury's Norman grid street plan makes this attractive Suffolk town easy to explore. It takes its name from the 9th-century East Anglian king. Following his murder by Danish raiders, his bones were buried in the abbey and the town became a place of pilgrimage. The town, with the abbey ruins at its heart, became wealthy on the wool trade in the Middle Ages and is still a lively agricultural town today. Among its many attractive buildings are Moyse's Hall, now a local museum and the Angel Hotel which features in Dicken's *Pickwick Papers*.
www.visit-suffolk.org.uk

➕ 6C 🛈 6 Angel Hill ☎ 01284 764667 ❹ Easter–Sep Mon–Sat 9.30–5.30, Sun 10–3; Oct–Easter Mon–Fri 10–4, Sat 9.30–1

CAMBRIDGE

Cambridge, and more particularly its world-renowned university, largely developed because of the persecution experienced by students at Oxford. They arrived in the 13th century and the University's oldest college dates from this time (Peterhouse, 1284). There are 31 colleges making up the modern University, the most recent being Robinson, added in 1977. Like Oxford (➤ 46–47), the town has benefited greatly from its academic connections. It is now the home of the 'Silicon Fen' – high-tech industries growing up in the flatlands that surround the city. The centre of Cambridge is all about its glorious buildings. King's College, famed for its magnificent 15th-century chapel and superb choir, forms one side of King's

Parade. A climb up the tower of Great St Mary's Church is rewarded with a view over the whole city. The oldest colleges, built around neat quadrangles, can easily be picked out. Further up a continuation of the same street stands Henry VIII's Trinity College. Between the colleges and the river lie the Backs, a series of genteel college gardens and lawns facing open fields across the water. You can hire the traditional punts to navigate the river. The biggest shopping area runs parallel to the colleges and is restrained in its modern use of the historic buildings. The botanic gardens and the outstanding collections in the **Fitzwilliam Museum** are also worth visiting.

www. visitcambridge.org

✚ 5C 🛈 Wheeler Street ☎ 0871 226 8006 🕓 Oct–Mar Mon–Fri 10–5.30, Sat 10–5; Easter–Sep Mon–Fri 10–5.30, Sat 10–5, Sun 11–4

Fitzwilliam Museum

✉ Trumpington Street ☎ 01223 332900 🕓 Tue–Sat 10–5, Sun 12–5
🎟 Free

CANTERBURY

Canterbury was a capital as long ago as the Iron Age, and a major Roman town. In AD 597, St Augustine founded the monastery, Christ Church, which became the first cathedral in England. Its magnificent Gothic successor, largely dating from the 12th century, is Canterbury's greatest treasure. Thomas à Becket was brutally murdered here in 1170, and his shrine became one of the most popular in Europe, second only to Rome – a pilgrimage immortalised by Chaucer in *The Canterbury Tales* (1388). Today the Archbishop of Canterbury is the head of the Church of England and leader of the worldwide Anglican community.

www.canterbury.co.uk

✚ 17Q 🛈 12/13 Sun Street, The Buttermarket ☎ 01227 378100;
🕓 Easter–Oct Mon–Sat 9.30–5; Nov–Easter 10–4

CHARTWELL

The home of Sir Winston Churchill from 1924 until the end of his life, Chartwell is an unpretentious Victorian country house, with stunning views over the Weald (➤ 157), and it became the place from which Sir Winston drew inspiration. The rooms remain much as he left them, with pictures, maps and personal mementoes that strongly evoke the career and wide-ranging interests of England's wartime prime minister. The beautiful terraced gardens contain his garden studio in which many of his paintings are displayed.

✠ 15Q ✉ Westerham, Kent ☎ 01732 866868; recorded information: 01732 868381 🌐 Apr–Jun Wed–Sun 11–5; Jul–Aug Tue–Sun 11–5; Sep–Oct Wed–Sun 11–5 🖐 Moderate 🍴 Restaurant (£–££)

CHILTERNS

The Chilterns are a range of chalk hills extending in a curve from Dunstable in the north to Reading in the south, characterized by their beech woodlands and pretty villages. Fingest is the prettiest of these, nestling in wooded downland with a Norman church and 18th-century inn. The area has been well protected from the advances of London's suburbia, but remains extremely accessible from the capital, with fast train and

tube links delivering you to the heart of this surprisingly quiet countryside. The western edge is marked by a chalkland ridge, traversed by the Ridgeway National Trail, itself following a prehistoric trade route, making excellent walking territory.

www.chilternaonb.org

14R Paul's Row, High Wycombe 01494 421892 Mon–Thu 9.30–5, Fri 9.30–4.30, Sat 9.30–4

DOVER CASTLE

Dover Castle is a formidable defensive structure, and was used as such from the 12th century until the 1980s. Overlooking the town, it has a massive keep built by Henry II in the 1180s, with walls 17–22ft (5–7m) thick. During the Civil War, the castle was seized by Oliver Cromwell. It was further strengthened during the Napoleonic Wars and played an important role in World War II. Dover's famous White Cliffs are honeycombed with fortifications used during this conflict. Admiralty Lookout in the castle grounds is a great place for views of the cliffs and across the Channel. The proximity to German guns on the French coast earned the defences the title 'Hellfire Corner'. In the town centre, **Dover Museum** tells the story of the development of the town and port, and includes the Dover Bronze Age Boat, a gallery with information on the Bronze Age.

www.english-heritage.org.uk

17P 01304 211067 Apr–Jul and Sep daily 10–6; Aug daily 9.30–6.30; Oct daily 10–5; Nov–Jan Thu–Mon 10–4; Feb–Mar daily 10–4

The Keep Restaurant (££) and The Tunnel Café (£–££)

Moderate–expensive

Dover Museum

Market Square, Dover 01304 20106; www.dover.gov.uk Mon–Sat 10–5.30, Sun 12–5 Inexpensive

ELY

Until the surrounding fens were drained, in the 17th century, the Isle of Ely was indeed an island, in the middle of a labyrinth of water-filled channels and overhanging foliage. So formidable a natural defence were the marshes, that those opposing the Norman invasion were able to do so until 1071. To mark their ultimate victory, the Normans built the massive 'Cathedral of the Fens', which towers above the low-lying land. Ely is an agreeable jumble of time-warped buildings dating from the 15th century to Georgian and Victorian times.

✚ 5C 🛈 Oliver Cromwell's House, 29 St Mary's Street ☎ 01353 662062
🕒 Apr–Oct daily 10–5.30; Nov–Mar Sun–Fri 11–4, Sat 10–5

HASTINGS

Hastings is known to every British schoolchild as the place where in 1066 the Norman Conquest of England began. By the time William of Normandy landed, Hastings was already a flourishing port. Today, it is a pleasing mixture of contemporary seaside resort, artists' retreat and a small fishing port. Look for the tall weatherboarded fishing-net stores, unique to the town.

Understandably, Hastings makes the most of the '1066' story, as they do at nearby Battle, 5 miles (8km) away, which boasts a magnificent abbey built to celebrate William's victory.

www.visithastings.com

✚ 16P 🛈 Queen's Square, Priory Meadow ☎ 0845 274 1001 ⏰ Mon–Fri 8.30–6.15, Sat 9–5, Sun 10.30–4.30

HEVER CASTLE

Once the home of Anne Boleyn, second wife of Henry VIII, and where Anne of Cleves, his fourth wife, lived after their divorce, Hever Castle is a fine, moated stronghold and contains many Tudor artefacts, paintings and other interesting objects. Having fallen into disrepair, the 13th-century castle was bought by William Waldorf Astor, the American millionaire owner of *The Observer* newspaper, who had it painstakingly restored, and, though the Astor family no longer owns it, the castle remains a splendid example of regal life in Tudor times.

www.hevercastle.co.uk

✚ 15P ✉ Hever, near Edenbridge, Kent ☎ 01732 865224 ⏰ Castle: Mar–Oct daily 12–5; Nov daily 12–3.30. Gardens: Mar–Oct daily 11–5, Nov daily 11–3.30. Closed Dec–Feb ✋ Expensive 🍴 The Moat and the Pavilion restaurants (£–££)

LEEDS CASTLE

Originally a Saxon royal manor built in AD857, Leeds Castle, which in its present form was begun in 1120, became the home of the Norman Crevecouer family and later a royal palace during the reign of Edward I. The castle, which rises fairy tale-like from a lake, has been the home of six medieval queens, and is a delightful place to visit. If you're travelling out from London Victoria, buy an all-inclusive rail ticket to Bearsted, which includes coach shuttle and entry to the castle. www.leeds-castle.com

🚩 16P ✉ Leeds, near Maidstone, Kent ☎ 01622 76540 🕓 Apr–Sep daily 10–5; Oct–Mar daily 10–3 ✋ Expensive 🍴 The Fairfax Hall (£–££) and The Terrace Room (££)

LULLINGSTONE ROMAN VILLA

The villa was only discovered in 1939, and ranks as one of the major archaeological finds of the 20th century. It was built around AD100, and was in use throughout the Roman occupation. Much of the villa's layout is visible, as are a number of mosaic floors.

🚩 16Q ✉ Lullingstone Lane, Eynsford, Dartford, Kent ☎ 01322 863467 🕓 Apr–Sep daily 10–6; Oct–Nov and Feb–Mar daily 10–4; Dec–Jan Wed–Sun 10–4 🍴 Eynsford village ✋ Inexpensive

NORFOLK BROADS

Flowing through the heart of Norfolk is a spread of waterways known as 'The Broads', an area of slow-flowing rivers – the Yare,

Waveney, Bure Ant and Thurne – and shallow lakes, 42 in all, that were created by the extraction of peat, and subsequent flooding, several hundred years ago. Sailing and cruising on the Broads are popular pursuits, and the wildlife on the Broads is second to none. The only efficient way of exploring the Broads is, of course, by boat, and you could easily spend many days here meandering around over 130 miles (200km) of lock-free, navigable waterways.
www.broads-authority.gov.uk

✚ 18T ℹ Station Road, Hoveton ☎ 01603 782281 🕐 Apr–Nov daily 9–5

NORWICH

Whatever your interests the market city of Norwich has something to offer – architecture, art, museums, leisure activities or simply shopping. The slender-spired cathedral, surrounded by cobbled streets with fine old buildings, and the bustling, modern shopping centres are all dominated by a Norman castle, built around 1160, which itself houses a fine museum. Norwich is particularly well endowed with medieval churches (though not all are still in use), notably St John Maddermarket, which contains a fine collection of monumental brasses and St Michael at Plea, which takes its name from the archdeacon's court.

Undoubtedly a wealthy medieval city, Norwich is still East Anglia's unofficial capital, and a useful base from which to explore the Broads and the beautiful Norfolk coastline.

www.visitnorwich.co.uk

✚ 18T ℹ The Forum, Millenium Plain ☎ 01603 727927 ◷ Apr–Oct Mon–Fri 9.30–5.30, Sat 9.30–6; Nov–Mar Mon–Sat 9.30–5.30

PENSHURST PLACE

The delightful village of Penshurst lies at the confluence of the rivers Eden and Medway and is dominated by 14th-century Penshurst Place. The finest privately owned manor house in Kent, it was the birthplace of Sir Philip Sidney (1554–86), the English

poet and Elizabethan soldier. The massive chestnut roof of the Barons Hall in Penshurst Place, built by Sir John de Pulteney, four times Mayor of London, is its most spectacular feature. The house is set in magnificent formal gardens.

www.penshurstplace.com

✚ 16P ✉ Penshurst, near Tonbridge, Kent ☎ 01892 870307; 🕐 House: Mar–Nov daily 12–4. Grounds: Mar–Nov daily 10.30–6 ✋ Moderate 🍴 Garden Restaurant (£–££)

ROCHESTER

Rochester, known jointly with neighbouring Chatham as the Medway Towns, was founded by the Romans at the point where their great road from the Channel ports, Watling Street, crossed the River Medway. Later, in AD604, the Saxons founded a cathedral here, the second oldest in England, and on that was rebuilt by the Normans. They also built a fine castle here, recognizing the city's strategic importance.

Many of the buildings in Rochester are Georgian and there is a pleasant intimacy about the place, which would have appealed greatly to novelist Charles Dickens, who featured it in a number of his books, notably *Great Expectations*.

www.medway.gov.uk/tourism

✚ 16Q ℹ️ 95 High Street ☎ 01634 843666 🕐 Mon–Fri 9–5, Sat 10–5, Sun 10.30–5

SAFFRON WALDEN

This old market town's numerous timber-framed houses are a particular delight, many adorned with fine examples of the decorative plasterwork known as pargeting. There is a maze of medieval alleyways around the marketplace, and book and antique shops along Church Street. Until the 18th century, this was the main centre for growing the saffron crocus and the wealth from the trade helped build the magnificent church of St Mary the Virgin.

www.uttlesford.gov.uk/tourism
🕇 5C 🚹 1 Market Place, Market Square ☎ 01799 510444 🕓 Apr–Oct, Mon–Sat 9.30–5.30, Sun 10.30–1; Nov–Mar Mon–Sat 10–5

ST ALBANS

According to tradition, Alban was a Roman soldier who converted to Christianity, and was tortured and beheaded because of his refusal to sacrifice to pagan gods. He became England's first Christian martyr, and the abbey, founded here by King Offa of Mercia in the 8th century on the site of his martyrdom, rose to be one of the wealthiest in the country. Its massive stone gateway still stands to the west of the cathedral.

St Alban's today is a thriving shopping and business centre, but it has always held an important position as a staging post on the highway to London from the north, and remains popular with visitors and pilgrims. To the south of the town, the **Gardens of**

the Rose, with over thirty thousand specimens, is the world's largest rose collection.

www.stalbans.gov.uk

✚ 15R 🛈 Town Hall, Market Place ☎ 01727 864511; 🕐 Mon–Sat 10–5, Sun 10–4

Gardens of the Rose

☎ 01727 850461 🕐 Jun–Sep Mon–Sat 10–5, Sun 10–6 ✋ Moderate

SEVEN SISTERS

The country park that includes this famous landmark provides some of the finest coastal and riverside walking in the country, notably along the serpentine River Cuckmere into which the Seven Sisters finally slip. The Seven Sisters themselves are a stunning switchback of vertical chalk cliffs between Cuckmere Haven and Birling Gap.

www.sevensisters.org.uk

✚ 16N 🛈 Seven Sisters Country Park, Exceat, Seaford, East Sussex ☎ 01323 870280 🕐 Easter–Oct Mon–Fri 10.30–4.30, Sat–Sun 10.30–5; Nov–Easter weekends only 11–4

SUFFOLK COAST AND HEATHS

From its gently curving beaches to expansive wild heaths, reedbeds and wide estuaries, the Suffolk Coast and Heaths Area of Outstanding Natural Beauty is a stunning but fragile landscape. It extends roughly from Kessingland in the north to Aldeburgh. The coast is especially treasured for its wealth of wildlife and there is a splendid marshland bird reserve at Minsmere between Southwold and Leiston. On a different tack, Aldeburgh is famed for its June **arts festival** begun in 1948 by composer Benjamin Britten and tenor Peter Pears.

www.suffolkcoastandheaths.co.uk

✚ 18R

Aldeburgh Festival of Music and Arts

✉ Snape Maltings, (3 miles/5km inland) ☎ Box Office: 01728 687110; www.aldeburgh.co.uk

WALMER CASTLE

Intended to withstand the assaults of the French and Spanish following Henry VIII's break with the Roman Catholic Church, Walmer Castle has an original design (gunpowder had suddenly become a new threat) that is low and squat with massively thick walls. Later the castle was transformed into a stately home and became used as the residence of the Lord Warden of the Cinque Ports; the former Lord Warden's include Pitt the Younger, the Duke of Wellington and Sir Winston Churchill.

🚩 17P ✉ Kingsdown Road, Walmer, Kent ☎ 01304 364288
🕐 Apr–Sep daily 10–6; Oct Wed–Sun 10–4; Mar daily 10–4 👐 Moderate
🍴 Tea room (£–££)

WEALD

A varied and fascinating landscape between the chalkland scenery of the North and South Downs. Its name comes from the Old English word for woodland; the whole area was densely forested during Anglo-Saxon times. It became important for iron production before the industrial revolution. The **open air museum** at Singleton is England's leading museum of historic buildings and traditional rural life.

www.highweald.org

🚩 16P

Weald and Downland Open Air Museum

✉ Singleton, near Chichester ☎ 01243 811348; www.wealddown.co.uk
🕐 Jan to mid-Feb Wed, Sat, Sun 10.30–4; mid-Feb to Mar daily 10.30–4; Apr–Oct daily 10.30–6; Nov to mid-Dec daily 10.30–4 👐 Moderate

WINDSOR

The handsome market town of Windsor boasts the largest castle in England, within the bounds of which is something approaching another small, walled town. The attractive streets, many of them cobbled, have numerous Georgian and timber-framed houses and an outstanding Guildhall, designed by Sir Christopher Wren. The town is, of course, dominated by **Windsor Castle,** which is still occupied by the Queen. Work started on the castle in the 11th century, though most of the buildings are 12th century and were altered both in the 19th century, and in the 20th, following a disastrous fire in 1992. Across the Thames is the famous and exclusive Eton School.
www.windsor.gov.uk

✚ 14Q 🛈 Windsor Royal Shopping Centre ☎ 01753 743900
🕓 Apr–Jun Mon–Fri and Sun 10–4, Sat 10–5; Jul–Aug Mon–Sat 10–5.30, Sun 10–5; Sep Mon–Sat 10–5, Sun 10–4; Oct–Mar Mon–Fri and Sun 10–4, Sat 10–5

Windsor Castle

☎ 020 7766 7304 🕓 Mar–Oct daily 9.45–5.15; Nov–Feb daily 9.45–4.15
✋ Expensive

WOBURN ABBEY

The palatial 18th-century mansion of Woburn Abbey contains a fine private collection of art including pieces by Van Dyck, Canaletto, Gainsborough, Rembrandt and Velazquez, as well as some exquisite porcelain. A large part of the parkland forms the **Woburn Safari Park,** the largest drive-through reserve in Britain.
www.woburnabbey.co.uk

✚ 4C ✉ Woburn ☎ 01525 290666 🕓 Late Mar–late Sep Mon–Sat 11–4, Sun and public hols 11–5; early–late Oct and late Dec–late Mar Sat–Sun and public hols 11–4 🍴 Flying Duchess Pavilion (££)
✋ Expensive

Woburn Safari Park

☎ 01525 290407; www.woburnsafari.co.uk 🕓 Mar–Oct daily 10–5

around the South Downs

a drive

Leave Chichester by heading north on the A286 for Midhurst, but just after Mid Lavant turn onto the B2141, following a delightful route through wooded downland to Chilgrove and South Harting.

Chilgrove is little more than a handful of cottages and a pub in a richly green valley, dotted with isolated farms; there are the remains of two Roman villas near by.

Just as the B-road leaves South Harting, turn right onto a minor road to East Harting, Elsted and Lower Elsted and,

ultimately, meet the A272 at Stedham Common. Turn right and shortly left for the hamlet of Iping, where you cross the River Rother.

Iping is an attractive Downs village of old cottages, a mill and a five-arched bridge spanning the river. Stedham Common is scattered with prehistoric burial mounds.

A short way further on, turn right and follow country lanes towards Easebourne. When you meet the A286, turn right and go into Midhurst.

Midhurst is a busy market town with a wide, spacious

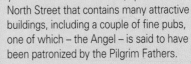

North Street that contains many attractive buildings, including a couple of fine pubs, one of which – the Angel – is said to have been patronized by the Pilgrim Fathers.

In the centre of Midhurst, where the road makes a pronounced bend, look for the turning, on the right, to Bepton and follow this to a T-junction, near the hamlet. Turn left to Cocking, a roadside village in a wooded gap. Continue to follow the A286 to West Dean, a lovely place with lots of flint cottages. From West Dean, stay on the main road to return to Chichester.

Distance 55 miles (88km)
Time 2–3 hours plus stops
Start/end point Chichester ✚ 14P
Lunch There are country pubs in Chilgrove, South Harting, Elsted, Lower Elsted, Easebourne, Midhurst, Cocking and West Dean

HOTELS

Beauport Park Hotel (££)

A Georgian country house set in parkland with its own swimming pool, tennis courts, putting green, candle-lit restaurant and open log fires; close to 18- and 9-hole golf courses.

✉ Battle Road, Hastings, East Sussex ☎ 01424 851222

Drakes (££–£££)

This hip boutique hotel on the seafront has 20 rooms and is best for those wanting to explore Brighton's lively nightlife.

✉ 43–44 Marine Parade, Brighton ☎ 01273 696934;
www.drakesofbrighton.com

Gravetye Manor (£££)

See pages 72–73.

The Old Bridge Hotel (££)

The ultimate country hotel in a town. The lounges here extend into a really splendid conservatory where you can enjoy brasserie-style food or visit the top-class restaurant; all rooms are elegantly and comfortably furnished.

✉ The High Street, Huntingdon, Cambridgeshire ☎ 01480 424300

The Norfolk Mead Hotel (££)

Near Norwich and the Norfolk Broads, the hotel stands in secluded grounds by the River Bure, and has an excellent restaurant.

✉ Church Loke, Coltishall, near Norwich, Norfolk ☎ 01603 737531

Ravenwood Hall Hotel (££)

Set in 7 acres of woodland and landscaped gardens just outside Bury St Edmunds, this is a hotel of character and quality; all the bedrooms are spaciously designed and thoughtfully equipped, and the welcoming restaurant provides a fixed-price menu. Outdoor heated pool.

✉ Rougham, Bury St Edmunds, Suffolk ☎ 01359 270345

York House Hotel (££)

Situated in a spectacular seafront setting, this hotel offers a high standard of accommodation, good food and wine, and a heated indoor swimming pool.

✉ 14–22 Royal Parade, Eastbourne, East Sussex ☎ 01323 412918

RESTAURANTS

Augustine's (££)

Popular restaurant in the centre of town serving modern European cuisine.

✉ 1 and 2 Longport, Canterbury, Kent ☎ 01227 453063 🕓 Daily 12–1.30, 6.30–9

The Crooked Barn (££)

Described as Oulton Broad's hidden oasis, this 18th-century thatched barn is a magnificent place to dine. The style of cuisine is 'New World' with excellent set menu lunches.

✉ Ivy House Farm Hotel, Ivy Lane, Oulton Broad, Lowestoft, Suffolk ☎ 01502 501353 🕓 Daily 12–1.30, 7–9.30

The Jolly Sportsman (£–££)

See page 58.

The Old Fire Engine House (££)

Owned and run by the same family for 30 years, this is an 18th-century building with a large walled garden and informal atmosphere. The cooking is based on local ingredients.

✉ 25 St Mary's Street, Ely, Cambridgeshire ☎ 01353 662582 🕓 Mon–Sat lunch, dinner, Sun lunch; closed for two weeks over Christmas

The Orangery (£££)

Modern English cooking served with skill in a delightful Georgian setting. Eating here gives a distinct feeling of being in a typical country home.

✉ Congham Hall Country House Hotel, Grimston (near King's Lynn), Norfolk ☎ 01485 600250 🕓 Daily 12–1.45, 7–9.15

Tatlers (££)

Brasserie-style restaurant in a converted Georgian townhouse serving modern British cuisine with a French twist.

✉ 21 Tombland, Norwich, Norfolk ☎ 01603 766670 ⊘ Mon–Sat 12–2, 6.30–10

Terre à Terre (££)

Exciting vegetarian restaurant in the centre of Brighton with organic wine and beer also on the menu.

✉ 71 East Street, Brighton, East Sussex ☎ 01273 729051 ⊘ Daily 12–3, 6–10.30; closed Tue lunch, 24–26 Dec, 1 Jan

ENTERTAINMENT

Arts Theatre

Cambridge's main theatre, which launched the careers of actors such as Stephen Fry and Derek Jacobi, provides an eclectic range of productions.

✉ 6 St Edward's Passage, Cambridge ☎ 01223 503333

Bournemouth International Centre

Three venues in one in this popular resort town.

✉ Exeter Road, Bournemouth ☎ 08701 113000

Chichester Festival Theatre

Classic and contemporary theatre.

✉ Oaklands Park, Chichester, W.Sussex ☎ 01243 781312; www.cft.org.uk

Komedia

Alternative theatre and stand-up comedy.

✉ 14–17 Manchester Street, Brighton

Norwich Arts Centre

One of East Anglia's top venues for the performing arts. A varied programme of comedy, art, dance, theatre and music from international names and new talent.

✉ Reeves Yard, off St Benedict's Street, Norwich ☎ 01603 660352; www.norwichartscentre.co.uk

Southwest England

The Southwest, also known as the West Country, reaches from Gloucester on the River Severn all the way to Land's End, and has some of the most naturally beautiful tracts of countryside anywhere in England. Here leafy lanes and flowering hedgerows pattern rolling green hills and link picture-postcard villages with thatched cottages, stately homes, riverside pubs and prehistoric sites that tell so much of England's heritage.

Two great national parks, Dartmoor and Exmoor, which provide wide, open spaces and the chance to escape and unwind, and these are supplemented by a string of Areas of Outstanding Natural Beauty and England's newest national park in the New Forest. Above all, the Southwest is a land of rich pastures that produce some of Englands' finest meat, cheeses and milk, it is also a top cider-producing area, able to boast cider of national and international reputation.

AVEBURY

The village of Avebury stands largely within a stone circle that rivals Stonehenge though the individual stones are smaller. An enormous earthwork encloses the main circle, which is thought to have been built around 2500BC. On first impressions it is difficult to grasp what this UNESCO World Heritage Site is about, but this is partially rectified by the **Alexander Keiller Museum** at the west entrance.

✚ 13Q ⊛ Stone Circle: daily

Alexander Keiller Museum

☎ 01672 539250 ⊛ Apr–Oct daily 10–6; Nov–Mar daily 10–4 🍴 In village (£) 🖐 Inexpensive

BATH

See pages 36–37.

BRISTOL

Bristol ensured its place as an inland port to rival London from the Middle Ages, when its wealth grew on the trade in slaves, cocoa, sugar, tobacco and manufactured goods between the New World and Africa. Many of the buildings from this period were damaged during World War II, though some remain intact.

In the 19th century, the engineer Brunel created two of the city's

most famous monuments, the *SS Great Britain*, the world's first ocean-going steamship with screw propulsion, and the spectacular

Clifton Suspension Bridge, a magnificent structure high above the Avon Gorge. The docks have been redeveloped and now offer eateries, family attractions and museums.
www.visitbristol.co.uk

🚆 11Q 🛈 The Annexe, Wildscreen Walk, Harbourside ☎ 0906 7112191 🕒 Mon–Fri 10–5, Sat–Sun 10–6

BUCKLAND ABBEY

Concealed in a secluded valley above the River Tavy, Buckland used to be a small but prominent Cistercian monastery. The house incorporates the ruins of the 13th-century abbey church, and has strong connections with the explorer Sir Francis Drake and his rival, Sir Richard Grenville.
www.nationaltrust.org.uk

🚆 9P ✉ Yelverton ☎ 01822 853607 🕒 Feb to mid-Mar Sat, Sun 2–5; mid-Mar to Oct Fri–Wed 10.30–5.30; Nov Sat–Sun 2–5; 2 Dec to mid-Dec Sat–Sun 11–5 💷 Moderate 🍴 Restaurant and tea room (£–££)

CHEDDAR GORGE

Slicing through the Mendip Hills, this limestone gorge is an impressive and beautiful natural phenomenon. The road through the gorge runs for about 2 miles (3.2km) and, at its narrowest, passes below cliffs almost 500ft (152m) high. Beneath the gorge the **Cheddar Caves** were fashioned by subterranean rivers during the last Ice Age, and were later occupied by prehistoric man.

✚ 110 ℹ The Gorge, Cheddar
✉ 01934 744071

Cheddar Caves

☎ 01934 472343; www.cheddarcaves.co.uk
🕐 Jul–Aug 10–5.30; Sep–Jun 10.30–5
✋ Expensive 🍴 Café

CHELTENHAM

The spa town of Cheltenham, well known for its racecourse and its ladies' college, is an excellent place from which to explore the Cotswolds. Most visitors come here today for the architecture rather than for the waters. The town suffers from unimaginative planning that sprinkles shopping centres in among attractive squares, gardens and elegant, Regency-period buildings. Ironically, the civic offices are one of the best features of Cheltenham, and a most delightful thoroughfare. The **Pittville Pump Room,** a mile from the town centre, in an area of villas and parkland, is one of the town's finest examples of the Regency style, constructed as a spa and social centre for Joseph Pitt's new estate. The **Art Gallery and Museum** has sections covering William Morris, the English craftsman, poet and socialist, and the Arts and Crafts Movement, which sprang from his association with pre-Raphaelite colleagues. Lovers of music will want to visit No.4 Clarence Road

where composer Gustav Holst, best known for *The Planets*, was born. Displays include Holst memorabilia and descriptions of life in the 19th and early 20th century.
www.visitcheltenham.com

➕ 2C 🅸 The Promenade ✉ 01242 522878 🕓 Mon–Sat 9.30–5.15

Pittville Pump Room

✉ Pittville Park ☎ 01242 523852 ✋ Free

Art Gallery and Museum

✉ Clarence Street ☎ 01242 237431; www.cheltenhammusuems.org.uk
🕓 Mon–Sat 10–5.20 ✋ Free

COTEHELE HOUSE

Leaning into the hillside above the River Tamar, Cotehele was mainly built between 1485 and 1627, and was, for centuries, the home of the Edgcumbe family. This is a small and fragile house; consequently visitor numbers are limited to 80 at any one time, so be prepared to wait for entry. The house contains tapestries and original furniture and armour, but if you have to wait, the formal gardens, which overlook a valley garden, will agreeably pass your time.

➕ 9P ✉ St Dominick, near Saltash ☎ 01579 351346; information line: 01579 352739 🕓 House: mid-Mar to Sep Sat–Thu 11–4.30; Oct Sat–Thu 11–4. Garden: daily 10.30–dusk ✋ Moderate 🍴 The Barn café (£)

THE COTSWOLDS

See pages 38–39.

DARTMOOR

Wild, bleak, high and windswept, Dartmoor is the only true wilderness in southern England. It occupies the main part of the country between Exeter and Plymouth, and has a 'grim charm', alluded to by Sir Arthur Conan Doyle in *The Hound of the Baskervilles*. But it has a distinct beauty too, that should compel everyone to cross its barren moors at least once. That prehistoric people found it less forbidding is evidenced by the scattered remnants of Stone and Bronze Age presence. The remains of tin and copper mining are also to be found here, the museum at **Morwellham Quay** is a fascinating place to learn about this aspect of the region's history. Dartmoor has been a protected **national park** since 1951.

✚ 9P

Morwellham Quay

✉ Morwellham ☎ 01822 832766; www.morwellham-quay.co.uk
🕐 Apr–Oct daily 10–5.30; Nov–Mar daily 10–4.30 💷 Moderate

Dartmoor National Park

ℹ High Moorland Visitor Centre, Tavistock Road, Princetown ☎ 01822 890414; www.dartmoor-npa.gov.uk 🕐 Daily 10–5; winter daily 10–4

DORCHESTER

For lovers of Thomas Hardy's works, this is the place to visit – he was born just three miles away at Higher Bockhampton. Hardy worked as an architect in the town, and his novel, *The Mayor of Casterbridge*, describes the town as it was in the mid-19th century. The High Street is particularly handsome, and boasts a variety of Georgian town houses. The 18th-century Shire Hall contains the old county court, preserved as a memorial to the Tolpuddle Martyrs who were tried here in 1834.

www.westdorset.com

✚ 11P ℹ 11 Antelope Walk ☎ 01305 267992 🕐 Apr–Oct Mon–Sat 9–5, Sun 10–3; Oct–Apr Mon–Sat 9–4

EDEN PROJECT

A gateway into the world of plants, the Eden Project recreates climates of the world inside two gigantic 'biodomes' – futuristic conservatories. Situated in a former clay quarry, the biodomes re-create different climates enabling visitors to wind their way through plants from places such as the Amazon, West Africa, Malaysia, the Mediterranean, South Africa and California.

www.edenproject.com

✚ 8N ✉ Bodelva, St Austell ☎ 01726 811911 ⏱ Mar–Oct daily 10–6; Nov–Feb 10–4.30 ✋ Expensive 🍴 Café

EXETER

Exeter, the charming county town of Devon, has a commanding position on the River Exe. The town's most distinguished feature is its cathedral, a superb architectural masterpiece enhanced by two great Norman towers that flank the nave. Inside you'll find the longest unbroken Gothic ceiling in the world, a stunning bishop's throne and misericords that are thought to be the oldest in the country, dating from 1260.
www.exeter.gov.uk

🚻 10P 🅿 Civic Centre, Paris Street ☎ 01392 265700 🕓 Mon–Sat 9–5; summer Mon–Sat 9–5, Sun 10–4

EXMOOR

See pages 40–41.

FROME

Lying at the eastern end of the Mendip Hills, Frome (pronounced 'froom') is a picturesque collection of steep cobbled streets, weavers' cottages, Georgian houses, old shops

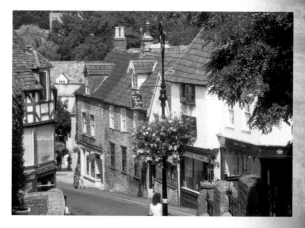

and a thriving market. The town's prosperity was founded on cloth making, chiefly from the medieval period to the end of the 18th century. Catherine Hill and Gentle Street are worth exploring and the congregational chapel on Rook Lane is particularly fine.

www.frometouristinfo.co.uk

✚ 120 🛈 The Round Tower, 2 Bridge Street ☎ 01373 467271 🕔 Mon–Sat 10–4.30 or 5

GLASTONBURY

Glastonbury was a centre of the early Christian church and lies at the heart of the mystical Isle of Avalon. Stories abound of the Holy Grail, King Arthur and the miraculous Glastonbury Thorn, said to have sprouted from the staff of Joseph of Arimathea. There are abbey ruins and a tower crowning the evocative Tor, a conical hill rising above the Somerset Levels, but these days the area is best known for the vast summer music **festival** at nearby Pilton. To the south, the Jacobean Montacute House, near Yeovil, displays important works from the National Portrait Gallery.

www.glastonburytic.co.uk

✚ 110 🛈 9 High Street BA6 9DP ☎ 01458 832954 🕔 Sun–Thu 10–5, Fri, Sun 10–5.30; (sometimes closed 1–2)

Glastonbury Festival

www.glastonburyfestivals.co.uk

GLOUCESTER

From Roman origins, Gloucester became a major port on the River Severn, until difficulties of navigation shifted the focus of trade to Bristol, substantially downstream. The docks, which had

developed following the opening of the Sharpness Canal in 1827, declined too, but in recent years have seen a revival, and are now a vigorous and vast commercial enterprise – especially if you're looking for antiques. The pride of Gloucester, however, is its enormous cathedral, which has huge Norman columns, and the tomb of Edward II. Gloucester's lively streets are bustling with shops, pubs and businesses, but all are noticeably lower key than those at nearby Cheltenham.

www.gloucester.gov.uk/tourism

✚ 2C 🛈 28 Southgate Street ☎ 01452 396572 ⏲ Mon–Sat 10–5

ISLE OF WIGHT

Known locally as 'The Island', the Isle of Wight packs a great scenic punch. It has a mild climate, and though it is only just off the Hampshire coast, its remoteness has attracted many famous visitors, including Tennyson, Charles Dickens and Queen Victoria, who built a retreat for her family at **Osborne,** and lived here after Prince Albert died. Not surprisingly, the island has a good deal of Victoriana, it also has beautiful, unspoiled countryside, much like Southern England without the traffic, and a varied and impressive coastline, with chalk stacks (the Needles – best seen as you approach by ferry from France) and sandy beaches.

www.islandbreaks.co.uk

✚ 13N 🛈 81–83 Union Street, Ryde ☎ 01983 813818 ◷ Mid-Apr to Nov Mon–Sat 9.30–5, Sun 10–4

Osborne House

✉ 1 mile (1.6km) east of Cowes ☎ 01983 200022 ◷ Apr–Sep daily 10–5; Oct daily 10–4; prebooked tours: Nov–Mar Wed–Sun 10–4

✋ Expensive

LANHYDROCK HOUSE

Lanhydrock House is a fascinating late 19th-century house, full of period atmosphere and the trappings of a high Victorian country house. The gatehouse and north wing survive from the 17th century, but the rest of the house was rebuilt following a fire in 1881. The gardens are famously beautiful.

www.nationaltrust.org.uk

✚ 8P ✉ Lanhydrock, near Bodmin ☎ 01208 265950 ◷ House: mid-Mar to Sep Tue–Sun 11–5.30; Oct Tue–Sun 11–5. Gardens: all year daily 10–6

✋ Moderate 🍴 Restaurant and café (£–££)

LONGLEAT

Longleat House is a vast Elizabethan mansion, with 19th-century interiors and numerous tourist attractions, not least lions, sea-lions, a railway and the world's longest hedge maze. The house has been the home of the Thynne (or Thynn) family for more than 450 years, and is now lived in by the 7th Marquess of Bath and his family. As well as providing visitor attractions, Longleat also plays an important role in the world programme of the breeding and conservation of endangered species.

www.longleat. co.uk

➕ 12Q ✉ Warminster ☎ 01985 844400 🕐 Apr to early Nov, daily 10 or 11–4 or 5.30 👛 Expensive 🍴 Cafés (£–££)

NEW FOREST NATIONAL PARK

The name of this vast special heritage area in southwest Hampshire is misleading. There is more heathland than woodland and it certainly isn't new. It's the remains of a primeval forest enclosed and protected by William the Conqueror, who used it as a deer-hunting reserve. Forest people still graze their animals and exercise ancient woodland rights that go back to the time of the Conquest. The main wooded area is around Lyndhurst, the so-called 'capital' of the Forest. In the south of the forest lies Beaulieu, a pretty village, most famous for the

National Motor Museum, with over 250 historic vehicles.

www.newforestnpa.gov.uk

✚ 13P ℹ New Forest Visitor Information Centre, High Street, Lyndhurst
☎ 023 8028 2269 ⏰ Mar–Jun, Sep–Oct Mon–Sun 10–5; Jul–Aug Mon–Sun
10–6; Nov–Feb Mon–Fri 10–4, Sat–Sun 10–5

National Motor Museum
✉ Beaulieu, Hampshire ☎ 01590 612345; www.beaulieu.co.uk
⏰ May–Sep daily 10–6; Oct–Apr daily 10–5

PORTSMOUTH

Occupying the peninsula of
Portsea Island, Portsmouth
is Britain's foremost naval
base. The Romans were
not slow to recognize the
strategic importance of this
position, and built a fortress
here. But it was only after
the Norman Conquest that
a peopled settlement
developed, and not until
Tudor times that the
position was fully exploited.
The Royal Naval Base on
Queen Street is where
you'll find the **Flagship
Portsmouth,** comprising
HMS *Warrior* 1860, HMS

Victory, the *Mary Rose*, the Royal Naval Museum, the Dockyard
Apprentice exhibition and the Warships by Water tour.
www.visitportsmouth.co.uk

✚ 14P ℹ Clarence Esplanade, Southsea ☎ 023 9282 6722 ⏰ Jul–Aug
daily 9.30–5.45; Sep–Jun daily 9.30–5.15

Flagship Portsmouth
✉ Historic Dockyard ☎ 023 9283 9766; www.flagship.org.uk ⏰ Apr–Oct
daily 10–5.30; Nov–Mar 10–5 👋 Moderate

ISLE OF PURBECK

Although not really an island, Purbeck certainly feels like one, jutting out into Poole Harbour. The best approach is by ferry from Sandbanks, from where the beautiful villages and the dramatic coastline can be explored quite easily on foot. Worth looking at are Wareham, Corfe Castle, Lulworth Cove and the limestone arch of Durdle Door. Swanage, the main town, is connected to Corfe by steam railway.

www.purbeck.gov.uk

➕ 12P 🛈 Purbeck Information and Heritage Centre, South Street, Wareham ☎ 01929 552740 🕓 Daily 10–5. Closed Sun in winter

ST IVES

Beautifully positioned, with sandy beaches flanking a rugged headland, St Ives is a small village of cobbled streets and steep alleyways. Its prosperity was founded on pilchards and tin mining, but the town now relies on tourism and art, having attracted many well-known artists including Barbara Hepworth, Naum Gabo and Roger Hilton. The **Barbara Hepworth Museum and Sculpture Garden** gives a detailed insight into the local arts scene. The **Tate Gallery,** overlooking Porthmeor Beach, also shows local work.

www.visit-westcornwall.com

➕ 7N 🛈 The Guildhall, Street-an-Pol ☎ 01736 796297 🕓 Jun–Sep Mon–Fri 9–5.30, Sat 9–5, Sun 10–4; Oct–May Mon–Fri 9–5, Sat 10–1

Barbara Hepworth Museum and Sculpture Garden

✉ Barnoon Hill ☎ 01736 796226 🕓 Mar–Oct daily 10–5.20; Nov–Feb Tue–Sun 10–4.20 ✋ Inexpensive

Tate Gallery

☎ 01736 796226; www.tate.org.uk/stives 🕓 Mar–Oct Mon–Sun 10–5.20; Nov–Feb Tue–Sun 10–4.20 ✋ Moderate 🍴 Café (£)

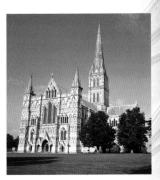

SALISBURY

England's finest cathedral city has grown since 1220, when the settlement moved from Old Sarum, an Iron-Age community just north of its present-day site. The cathedral, with its huge spire, was begun in 1220 and is entirely Early English in style. It is one of the finest medieval buildings in the country, and the Chapter House contains a copy of the Magna Carta. The city is a mix of medieval, Georgian and Victorian buildings and has no high-rise buildings to challenge the dominance of the cathedral.

www.salisbury.gov.uk/tourism

🕂 13P 🚹 Fish Row ☎ 01722 334956
⚄ Oct–Apr Mon–Sat 9.30–5; May Mon–Sat 9.30–5, Sun 10.30–4.30; Jun–Sep Mon–Sat 9.30–6, Sun 10.30–4.30

STONEHENGE

See pages 48–49.

TRURO

The county town of Cornwall was the main port for the export of tin, and became a medieval 'stannary' town, where tin was taken to be weighed and taxed. Little remains of Truro's ancient past, though there are numerous fine Georgian buildings, especially along Lemon Street. Completed in 1910, the cathedral was the first Anglican cathedral to be built since St Paul's in London, and incorporates parts of the earlier church that stood on the site.

www.truro.gov.uk

✚ 8N 🏛 Municipal Building, Boscawen Street ☎ 01872 274555;
🕐 Easter–May, Sep–Oct Mon–Fri 9–5.15, Sat 10–1; Jun–Aug Mon–Fri 9–6, Sat 10–5; Nov–Easter Mon–Thu 9–5.15, Fri 9–5.45

WELLS

The exquisite market place in this, England's smallest city, seems to have architecture from every conceivable period, including two medieval gatehouses, one of which leads to the splendid cathedral, the other to the Bishop's Palace.

The whole city seems to have altered little in 800 years, having

successfully hung on to its medieval character, and is a perfect place to spend a relaxing day, or use as a base from which to visit the Mendip Hills and Cheddar Gorge (➤ 168).

The cathedral, one of England's most beautiful, dates from the 12th century, and its most impressive feature is the ornate west front, although many visitors are fascinated by the mechanical clock dating from 1392, high up in the north transept. Cathedral Close is a cluster of attractive buildings with histories closely associated with the cathedral. A year-round programme of recitals provides the opportunity to hear a cathedral choir in full song.

www.wells.gov.uk

➕ 110 ℹ️ Town Hall, Market Place
☎ 01749 672552 🕐 Apr–Oct daily
9.30–5.30; Nov–Mar daily 10–4

WINCHESTER

Alfred the Great's Wessex capital was the capital of all England from the 10th century until the Norman Conquest. It is one of the greatest historic cities in the country. Twenty kings are buried here and it overflows with medieval and later buildings. So important was the city in the 11th century that William the Conqueror's coronation was held both in London and Winchester. It was the monks of Winchester that he commissioned to carry out his Domesday Survey. Winchester also enjoys literary links; Jane Austen lived at nearby Chawton and died in the city in 1817, and pioneer angler Isaak Walton fished the local waters and also died here in 1653.

www.visitwinchester. co.uk

➕ 13P ℹ️ Guildhall, The Broadway
☎ 01962 840500 🕐 Apr–Sep
Mon–Sat 9.30–5.30, Sun 11–4;
Oct–Mar Mon–Sat 10–5

a walk around the Lizard

A challenging walk through spectacular coastal scenery with lunch in a picturesque fishing village.

Head towards the lighthouse and soon go into the grounds of Polbrean Hotel, heading for the cliff path. Turn left along the path and follow it to Housel Bay. Continue round Bass Point.

The unused castellated building here was once a signal station.

At Kilcobben Cove go behind the lifeboat station and into Church Cove.

On the beach is a lifeboat station built at the end of the 19th century in such a way that the lifeboat had to be turned around ninety degrees before it could be launched; it didn't last.

Follow the coastal path to the Devil's Frying Pan, a large, collapsed cave, and go round the back of it to Inglewidden. Continue with the coastal path to Cadgwith, and go through the gardens of Hillside.

Cadgwith is a charming village on steep sea slopes, with lots of thatched cottages and buildings in the Serpentine rock for which the Lizard is famous.

Go back up to Hillside, but turn right in Prazegooth Lane. At the top, bear right to a road. Turn left, pass Gwavas

Jersey Farm and, when the road bends right, go forward onto a footpath. Head across a field to a marker pole, and up steps onto the top of a wall. At the other end take a concrete farm access road to Trethvas Farm, and turn left for the Lizard. Continue now across fields to the Lizard, and then head for the 'Most Southerly Point'. In so doing you will return to your starting point.

Distance 7.5 miles (12km)
Time 5 hours with stops, 3–4 hours without stopping
Start/end point Lizard lighthouse car park ✚ 7N
Lunch The Inn at Cadgwith (£–££)

HOTELS

The Ayrlington (££)

An elegant Victorian villa within a few minutes' walk of the Roman Baths and the city centre. The hotel, which overlooks the medieval abbey, offers an extensive range of facilities and quality accommodation.

✉ 24–25 Pulteney Road, Bath ☎ 01225 425495; www.ayrlington.com

Bovey Castle Hotel (££–£££)

See page 72.

Hatton Court (££)

Set 600ft (183m) above sea level on top of Upton Hill, this manor house provides sweeping views across the River Severn to the Malvern Hills. The emphasis here is on comfort, and bedrooms are elegantly furnished.

✉ Upton Hill, Upton St Leonards, Gloucester ☎ 01452 617412

The Idle Rocks Hotel (£–££)

With commanding views over the quayside in St Mawes, this comfortable Cornish retreat is excellently placed for local walks and has a good restaurant.

✉ Harbourside, St Mawes, Cornwall ☎ 01326 270771

Pedn Olva (££)

The many levels to this 30-room hotel make it seem like a ship moored in this arty little town. A comfortable, relaxed hotel, with an excellent restaurant.

✉ The Warren, West Porthminster Beach, St Ives, Cornwall ☎ 01736 796222

Stock Hill Country House Hotel (£££)

The hotel, which also boasts an outstanding restaurant, stands in 11 acres (4.5ha) of parkland and is surrounded by rare old trees – a haven of peace and tranquillity. Charm and detailed elegance are the hallmark of all the rooms.

✉ Stock Hill, Gillingham, Dorset ☎ 01747 823626

The Thistle Bristol (££)

Though very centrally situated, this refurbished hotel offers quiet accommodation and all modern amenities.

✉ Broad Street, Bristol ☎ 0870 333 9130

RESTAURANTS

Castle Hotel (£–££)

The Castle is something of a gastronomic institution in Somerset, and its 800-year history makes it the West Country's most enduring watering hole.

✉ Castle Green, Taunton, Somerset ☎ 01823 272671 ⏰ Daily lunch, dinner

Le Champignon Sauvage (££–£££)

Classic cooking from David Everitt-Matthias in his delightful blue-and-yellow-painted restaurant

✉ Suffolk Road, Cheltenham, Gloucestershire ☎ 01242 573449 ⏰ Tue–Sat lunch, dinner

Fifteen Cornwall (££)

Celebrity chef Jamie Oliver's latest venture brings the idea behind his London restaurant – training young chefs – to the seaside. Excellent food and stunning views over Watergate Beach.

✉ Watergate Bay, Cornwall ☎ 01637 861000 ⏰ Daily 8.30–9.30am, 12–2.30, 7-9.45

George & Dragon (££)

Award-winning pub specialising in fresh fish. Former national winners of the AA 'Best Seafood Pub'.

✉ High Street, Rowde, Wiltshire ☎ 01380 723053 ⏰ Tue–Sat 12–3, 7–10; Sun 12–4

The New Angel (££-£££)

Another celebrity chef has decamped to the west country: John Burton Race's restaurant is popular for his skillful cooking and seasonal, locally-sourced produce.

✉ The Harbour, Dartmouth, Devon ☎ 01803 839425 ⏰ Tue-Sun 9–11am, 12–2, 6.30–9.30 (closed Sun pm, Mon)

Riverside Restaurant (£–££)

A highly regarded seafood restaurant in the heart of the fishing village of West Bay. Vegetarian and other dishes available.

✉ West Bay, Bridport, Dorset ☎ 01308 422011 ⏰ Lunch, dinner; closed Sun pm, Mon and Dec–Feb

The Old Success Inn (£–££)

See page 58.

Pump Room (££)

See page 59.

Riverstation (££)

The conversion of the old river police station on the docks near Bristol's city centre has produced a light and airy building which houses a fine restaurant on the first floor and a deli/espresso bar at dock level, with balconies overlooking the water.

✉ The Grove, Bristol ☎ 0117 914 4434 ⏰ Deli: meals all day. Restaurant: daily 12–2.30, 6–10.30

The Seafood Restaurant (£££)

Rick Stein's popular restaurant is the place to go for inventive seafood; the set-price meals are good value. Non-fish options are also available.

✉ Riverside, Padstow, Cornwall ☎ 01841 532700 ⏰ Lunch, dinner Mon–Sun

Tanners Restaurant (££)

A historic 15th-century house where Pilgrim fathers ate their final meal in England. The modern menu has French and American influences.

✉ Prysten House, Finewell Street, Plymouth, Devon ☎ 01752 252001 ⏰ Lunch, dinner Tue–Sat

ENTERTAINMENT

Axiom Centre for the Arts
Features a wide range of fringe music and theatre.
✉ 57 Winchcombe Street, Cheltenham, Gloucestershire ☎ 01242 253183

Colston Hall
Bristol's main venue, promoting major names in classical and popular music and its own classical promenade concerts.
✉ Colston Street, Bristol ☎ 0117 922 3686

Everyman Theatre
Produces many shows from Shakespeare to stand-up comedy.
✉ Regent Street, Cheltenham, Gloucestershire ☎ 01242 572573

Exeter Phoenix
Hosts contemporary and thought-provoking drama, dance, live art and music productions
✉ Bradninch Place, Gandy Street, Exeter, Devon ☎ 01392 667080; www.exeterphoenix.org.uk

Glastonbury
Renowned for its music festival at the end of June in nearby Pilton, the biggest and best in the country, with big-name bands to up-and-coming groups.
☎ www.glastonburyfestivals.co.uk

St George's Bristol
Renowned for its fine acoustics, this music venue welcomes a diverse selection of musicians and artists – from classical and chamber music to jazz and international artists.
✉ Great George Street, off Park Street, Bristol ☎ 0845 4024001; www.stgeorgesbristol.co.uk

Theatre Royal
Drama and ballet are regularly featured at the Theatre Royal, which also has a separate studio for experimental works.
✉ Sawclose, Bath ☎ 01225 448844; www.theatreroyal.org.uk

Index

Acknowledgements

The Automobile Association would like to thank the following photographers, companies and picture libraries for their assistance in the preparation of this book. Abbreviations for the picture credits are as follows: (t) top; (b) bottom; (c) centre; (l) left; (r) right; (AA) AA World Travel Library

4l Malvern Hills, AA/H Palmer; **4c** Lord Mayor's Parade, AA/P Enticknap; **4r** York Minster, AA/P Bennett; **5l** Gravetye Manor, AA/T Souter; **5r** Hyde Park, AA/R Strange; **6/7** Malvern Hills, AA/H Palmer; **8/9** Castle Howard, AA/J Morrison; **10** Houses of Parliament, AA/W Voysey; **10/11t** Buckland in the Moor, AA/R Moss; **10/11c** Carlisle Cathedral, AA/P Bennett; **11bl** Woburn Safari Park, AA/M Birkitt; **11cr** Wedgwood Visitor Centre, AA/P Baker; **12c** Portland, AA/M Jourdan; **12bl** Cheddar Gorge Cheese Co., AA/C Jones; **12/13t** Branscombe, AA/P Baker; **12/13b** Sweetings Oyster Bar, AA/R Mort; **13** Cup of tea, Stockbyte Royalty Free Photos; **14** Covent Garden, AA/M Jourdan; **15cl** Bottle of wine & glasses, Stockbyte Royalty Free Photos; **15cr** Ritz Tea Rooms, AA; **16** Oxford Street, AA/M Jourdan; **16/17** Lincoln Cathedral, AA/C Coe; **18/19** Trooping the Colour, AA/T Woodcock; **19** Enginuity Museum, AA/M Haywood; **20/21**, Lord Mayor's Parade, AA/P Enticknap; **24** Henley Regatta, AA; **24/25** Chelsea Flower Show, AA/M Birkitt; **26** Eurostar train, AA/W Voysey; **26/27** Stanstead Airport, AA/J Miller; **28/29** Oxford Street, AA/M Jourdan; **29** Liverpool Street Station, AA/R Strange; **31** Branxton, AA/C Lees; **32** Policeman, AA/M Jourdan; **34/35** York Minster, AA/P Bennett; **36** Roman Baths & Bath Abbey, AA/M Birkitt; **36/37** Bath, AA/S&O Mathews; **38** Lower Slaughter, AA/R Doran; **38/39** Bibury, AA/T Souter; **40cl** Exmoor Animal Centre, AA/W Voysey; **40bl** Lynmouth, AA/C Jones; **41t** Dulverton, AA/A Lawson; **41b** Valley of the Rocks, AA/C Jones; **42/43** Housesteads, AA/C Lees; **43** Vercovicium, AA/J Beazley; **44/45** Ashness Bridge, AA/T Mackie; **45** Loughrigg Fell, AA/T Mackie; **46** Radcliffe Camera, AA/S&O Mathews; **46/47** Oxford, AA/A Lawson; **47** Ashmolean Museum, AA/S Day; **48/49** Stonehenge, AA; **50/51t** Tower of London, AA/S Gibson; **50/51b** Tower of London, AA/W Voysey; **52** York Minster, AA/P Bennett; **52/53** National Railway Museum, AA/R Newton; **53** York, AA/R Newton; **54** Linton Falls, AA/A Baker; **54/55** Pennine Way, AA/J Hopkins; **55** Wharfedale, AA; **56/57**, Gravetye Manor, AA/T Souter; **59** Bath Pump Room, AA/E Meacher; **61** Norfolk Wildlife Park, AA/H Williams; **62** Elderwater, AA/EA Bowness; **64/65** Hampton Court, AA/R Mort; **66/67** Coniston Water, AA/M Birkitt; **68** Hyde Park, AA/R Strange; **70** Taunton, AA/R Hall; **70/71t** Branscombe, AA/P Baker; **70/71b** Bath, AA/E Meacher; **71t** Boston, AA/P Baker; **71b** Bournemouth, AA/W Voysey; **72** Dorchester Hotel, AA/P Wilson; **73** Ludlow, AA/I Burgum; **74/75** Hyde Park, AA/R Strange; **77** Buckingham Palace, AA/M Jourdan; **78** British Museum, AA/M Jourdan; **79t** The Mall, AA/T Woodcock; **79b** Covent Garden, AA/M Trelawny; **80** Cutty Sark, AA/R Victor; **80/81** Hyde Park, AA/R Mort; **82tl** London Eye, AA/M Jourdan; **82c** Museum of London, AA/T Woodcock; **82/83** National Gallery, AA; **84/85** Natural History Museum, AA/ M Jourdan; **85** Royal Botanical Gardens Kew, AA/T Woodcock; **86** Science Museum, AA/J Tims; **86/87** St Paul's Cathedral, AA/T Woodcock; **87** Tate Gallery, AA/P Wilson; **88/89** Trafalgar Square, AA/J McMillan; **90/91** Victoria and Albert Museum, AA/G Wrona; **91** Westminster Abbey, AA/B Smith; **97** Hebden Bridge, AA/L Whitwam; **98** Alnwick Castle, AA/C Lees; **99** Carlisle, AA/P Bennett; **100/101** Fountains Abbey, AA/L Whitwam; **102** Haworth, AA/P Wilson; **102/103** Lindisfarne Castle, AA/C Lees; **104/105** Killhope Lead Mining Museum, AA/C Lees; **105** Leeds and Liverpool Canal, AA/T Marsh; **106** Liverpool, AA; **106/107** Levens Hall, AA/T Mackie; **107** Manchester, AA/C Molyneux; **108/109** North of England Open Air Museum, AA/J Beazley; **110/111** Richmond Castle, AA/P Baker; **111tr** Kelham Island Industrial Museum, AA/S Day; **111bl** Sheffield, AA/P Brown; **112** Skipton, AA/P Wilson; **112/113** Whitby, AA/R Newton; **117** Warwick Castle, AA; **118** Birmingham City Museum and Art Gallery, AA/V Greaves; **118/119** Blenheim Palace, AA; **119** Bridgnorth, AA/I Burgum; **120** Buxton, AA/P Baker; **120/121** Peak Cavern, AA/M Birkitt; **122** Chester, AA/C Jones; **122/123** Haddon Hall, AA/P Baker; **123** Hereford Cathedral, AA; **124** Ironbridge, AA/M Haywood; **126** Ludlow, AA/R Surman; **126/127** Ludlow Castle, AA/C Jones; **127** Lyme Park, AA/M Birkitt; **128** Malvern Priory, AA/C Jones; **128b** Wenlock Priory, AA/M Short; **128/129** Nottingham, AA/P Baker; **131** Sherwood Forest, AA/M Birkitt; **132** St Chads Church Shrewsbury, AA/C Jones; **132/133** Shrewsbury, AA/M Allwood-Coppin; **133** Stratford upon Avon, AA/J Wyand; **134/135** Tatton Park, AA; **135** Worcester, AA/S&O Mathews; **136/137** Bakewell, AA/P Baker; **141** Youlgreave, AA/J Hopkins; **142/143** Blickling Hall, AA; **143t** Bodiam Castle, AA/J Miller; **143b** Brighton, AA/P Brown; **144** Bury St Edmunds, AA/R Surman; **144/145** Cambridge, AA/M Birkitt; **146/147t** Chartwell, AA/P Baker; **146/147b** Midhurst, AA/S&O Mathews; **147** Dover Castle, AA/D Forss; **148** Ely Cathedral, AA/T Mackie; **148/149** Hastings, AA/W Voysey; **150t** Leeds Castle, AA/D Forss; **150c** Lullingstone, AA/S&O Mathews; **150/151** Norfolk Broads National Park, AA/A Baker; **152** Norwich Cathedral, AA/S&O Mathews; **152/153** Norwich, AA/T Souter; **154** Saffron Walden, AA/C Coe; **154/155** Seven Sisters, AA/C Coe; **156/157** Minsmere, AA/P Baker; **156** Southwold AA/T Mackie; **157** Weald and Downland Museum, AA/W Voysey; **158/159** Windsor, AA/W Voysey; **160/161** The Ridgeway Hackpen Hill, AA/B Johnson; **165** Hound Tor Dartmoor National Park, AA/P Baker; **166** Avebury, AA/W Voysey; **166/167** Clifton Suspension Bridge, AA/T Souter; **167** SS Great Britain Bristol, AA/S Day; **168/169** Cheddar Gorge, AA/C Jones; **169** Cotehele Mill, AA/A Lawson; **170** Dartmoor, AA/W Voysey; **170/171** Eden Project, AA/R Tenison; **172** Frome, AA/R Moss; **172/173** Glastonbury Tor, AA/C Jones; **174** Gloucester Cathedral, AA/S Day; **174/175** The Needles, AA/S McBride; **175** Lanhydrock House, AA/R Moss; **176c** Longleat Safari Park, AA/W Voysey; **176b** New Forest ponies, AA/T Souter; **176/177** Longleat, AA/S Day; **177** HMS Victory Portsmouth, AA/W Voysey; **178/179** Flying Scotsman Swanage, AA/D Jackson; **179c** Salisbury Cathedral, AA/ C Jones; **179r** Salisbury Cathedral, AA/S&O Mathews; **180** Wells Cathedral, S&O Mathews; **180/181** Winchester Cathedral, AA/S Day; **182/183** Lizard Point, AA/C Jones.

Every effort has been made to trace the copyright holders, and we apologise in advance for any accidental errors.

We would be happy to apply the corrections in the following edition of this publication.

Questionnaire

Dear Traveler

Your comments, opinions and recommendations are very important to us.
So please help us to improve our travel guides by taking a few minutes to
complete this simple questionnaire.

Send to: Essential Guides,
MailStop 64, 1000 AAA Drive, Heathrow, FL 32746–5063

Your recommendations...

We always encourage readers' recommendations for restaurants, nightlife
or shopping – if your recommendation is added to the next edition of the
guide, we will send you a FREE AAA Essential Guide of your choice.
Please state below the establishment name, location and your reasons for
recommending it.

_____

_____

_____

_____

_____

Please send me AAA Essential _____

About this guide...

Which title did you buy?

_____ **AAA Essential**

Where did you buy it? _____

When? __ __ / __ __

Why did you choose a AAA Essential Guide? _____

_____

_____

Did this guide meet with your expectations?

Exceeded ☐   Met all ☐   Met most ☐   Fell below ☐

Please give your reasons _____

_____

_____

_____

continued on next page...

Were there any aspects of this guide that you particularly liked? _____

_____

_____

_____

_____

_____

Is there anything we could have done better? _____

_____

_____

_____

_____

_____

About you...

Name (Mr/Mrs/Ms) _____

Address _____

_____

_____ **Zip** _____

Daytime tel nos. _____

Which age group are you in?

Under 25 ☐   25–34 ☐   35–44 ☐   45–54 ☐   55–64 ☐   65+ ☐

How many trips do you make a year?

Less than one ☐   One ☐   Two ☐   Three or more ☐

Are you a AAA member? Yes ☐   No ☐

Name of AAA club _____

About your trip

When did you book? m m / y y   **When did you travel?** m m / y y

How long did you stay? _____

Was it for business or leisure? _____

Did you buy any other travel guides for your trip? Yes ☐   No ☐

If yes, which ones? _____

_____

Thank you for taking the time to complete this questionnaire.

All information is for AAA internal use only and will not be distributed outside the organization to any third parties.